Prospect Research is a Verb

Fundraising is the Subject

Meredith Hancks
Cara Rosson

*Charity*Channel®
PRESS™

Prospect Research Is a Verb: Fundraising Is the Subject

One of the **In the Trenches**™ series
Published by
CharityChannel Press, an imprint of CharityChannel LLC
30021 Tomas, Suite 300
Rancho Santa Margarita, CA 92688-2128 USA
http://charitychannel.com

Print ISBN: 978-1-938077-20-3 | eBook ISBN: 978-1-938077-26-5

Library of Congress Control Number: 2013936628

13 12 11 10 9 8 7 6 5 4 3 2 1

Printed in the United States of America

This and most CharityChannel Press books are available at special quantity discounts for bulk purchases for sales promotions, premiums, fundraising, or educational use. For information, contact CharityChannel Press, 30021 Tomas, Suite 300, Rancho Santa Margarita, CA 92688-2128 USA. +1 949-589-5938

About the Authors

Meredith Hancks

Meredith is the director of Prospect Research and Management for Western Illinois University in Macomb, where she's been employed since 2007. Prior to her research career, she worked in annual giving at private liberal arts colleges in Minneapolis and Chicago. The part of this profession she enjoys most is the search for information and the subsequent ability to help frontline fundraisers be more successful in their work.

She currently serves as chair of the Best Practices in Prospect Development subcommittee for the Association of Advancement Services Professionals. This team of professionals is committed to identifying and articulating best practices in all areas of prospect research and prospect management, using many of the principles included in this book. Meredith recently joined the board of Association of Professional Researchers for Advancement (APRA)–Illinois to help with programming events in downstate Illinois and was appointed vice president in January 2013. As a member of CharityChannel, she has contributed several book reviews as a We Review panelist and authored one book for the **In The Trenches**™ Series, titled *Getting Started in Prospect Research*.

Outside of work, Meredith is at this writing a doctoral candidate at the University of Minnesota, completing a dissertation on conflict in higher education. She and her husband have twin toddler sons who keep them endlessly entertained and provide a wellspring of joy. Her favorite quote comes from Henry David Thoreau, "If one advances confidently in the direction of his dreams, and endeavors to live the life which he has imagined, he will meet with a success unexpected in common hours." Thus far, Meredith has experienced that to be true.

Cara Rosson

Cara spent almost ten years in prospect research for universities large and small. She started working for Lori Hood Lawson at Florida State University and "womaned" Bradley University's one-person research office for seven great years. She continues to do Internet research, but now as a freelance contractor.

She is constantly amazed at how many connections she builds, and friends she makes, on the Internet. And she gets out of her desk chair plenty because of it.

Outside of work, Cara tries, mostly in vain, to corral two boys and two basset hounds. She volunteers for spiritual, environmental, political, and theatrical causes on a far-more-than-regular basis.

Her favorite quote is from her favorite movie, *Annie Hall*, and the great Woody Allen, "It reminds me of that old joke—you know, a guy walks into a psychiatrist's office and says, hey doc, my brother's crazy! He thinks he's a chicken. Then the doc says, why don't you turn him in? Then the guy says, I would but I need the eggs. I guess that's how I feel about relationships. They're totally crazy, irrational, and absurd, but we keep going through it because we need the eggs." And she loves eggs.

Authors' Acknowledgments

We owe many thanks and much gratitude to our friends and colleagues in all realms of fundraising. It's a small and close-knit world, and we feel grateful to be a part of it along with you. Thank you for teaching us, learning with us, and allowing us to share our knowledge back with you.

Our never-ending thanks to Stephen Nill, founder and CEO of CharityChannel, who continues to give us the opportunity to share our knowledge with the fundraising world through written word.

Thank you also to the other editors involved with bringing this manual to publication: Bill Smith and Jill McLain. We appreciate your countless hours reading through permutations of the writing and offering suggestions and assistance to make it the best it could be.

Special thanks specifically to our friend and colleague Lori Hood Lawson, who has mentored and supported us over the years. Without you, this manuscript would definitely not have come about! We truly value your insights, knowledge, and friendship that you have shown to us individually and collectively as we embarked on this journey.

Cara would like to send a special thanks to her former colleagues at Bradley University, who offered their time and knowledge to her whenever she had questions for them.

And, most importantly, I, Meredith, must offer my most sincere gratitude to my husband Jeff and our children Anders and Torben for allowing me to embark on this journey yet again.

Publisher's Acknowledgments

This book was produced by a team dedicated to excellence; please send your feedback to editors@charitychannel.com.

We first wish to acknowledge the tens of thousands of peers who call charitychannel.com their online professional home. Your enthusiastic support for the **In the Trenches**™ series is the wind in our sails.

Members of the team who produced this book include:

Editors

Acquisitions Editor: Stephen Nill

Comprehensive Editor: Bill Smith

Copy Editor: Stephen Nill

Production

In the Trenches Series Design: Deborah Perdue

Layout Editor: Jill McLain

Proofreaders: Jill McLain, Stephen Nill, Bill Smith

Administrative

CharityChannel LLC: Stephen C. Nill, CEO

Marketing and Public Relations: John Millen

Contents

Foreword

When I finally got the chance to read this manual, I was on a flight—barely made it—from ATL to SJC to visit relatives prior to the Nonprofit Technology Conference. I had "settled" back into my middle seat for the five-hour flight and waited for the familiar ding that would allow me to turn on my "electronic device," which would allow me to read this manual on prospect research. What you now hold in your hands is about to change your life forever.

I started in prospect research in 1998 at the Florida State University Foundation, having just graduated from their School of Information Studies (aka Library Science) with my master's degree. Back then, I aced the testing for the interview to become a research analyst by being able to write select statements for Dialog files 26 and 234, just to name a few.

OK—so maybe it was more than my Dialog skills that produced a job offer. When I think back on it all, I had always been a "seek and find" type—naturally curious, willing to help, eager to learn through teaching and hands-on training. Seemed like a perfect fit for me—I would always have to learn something new, which for me is a MAJOR job requirement.

By the time I hired Cara, I had become assistant director of research, and we no longer tested Dialog knowledge. The Internet had become truly accessible by all, and there was no longer the argument (OK, justification) about who should have and who should not have access to the Internet on their office PCs.

Yes, data has come a long way, baby.

A very important point to be made here about data—data is just data. The focus of a prospect researcher—or analyst, or development information professional—should be to find data with a purpose—that purpose being to advance the relationship between the prospect and the mission of the nonprofit organization or educational institution. Or not. That is, do the interests and capacity of the prospect match the needs of the organization? If not, move on. It is our responsibility as fundraising professionals to be cognizant of being good stewards of our donors' contributions. Data for data's sake simply just sits there. Putting it in a manageable and usable context is paramount.

Now, back to my flight. I had attended a lunch meeting of local businesspeople and entrepreneurs in Tallahassee. This was invitation only, and as it just so happens, my husband David has always been an entrepreneur, and I, well, I've embraced my inner entrepreneur as a consequence of marriage. There was much discussed at this roundtable, and while it was primarily focused on management issues and challenges, I learned something new there too about a certain industry. And I, of course, wondered, "How is this data being aggregated?"

This is just how I think. Perhaps you are new to the profession, to the industry, to philanthropy as a sector. Perhaps you don't know just yet how much employment comes from this sector in the United States. (Hint: the nonprofit sector is the third largest sector in the United States in terms of employment.)

This is just how I think, after being involved for the past ~15 years now. I have made truly wonderful friends and colleagues throughout my time in this sector. If you added up all of those years of experience amongst my friends and colleagues, I believe it would come to about 1,247 years. No joke.

And now enter Meredith. I have had the true pleasure of getting to know Meredith via the AASP Best Practices Committee for Prospect Development. We have endured trying to make conference sessions about process and procedures interesting and informative. We have worked (and continue to do so) with numerous colleagues to compile best practices for every component a research office must tackle, often never meeting each other face to face. Please, do check out our endeavors on the AASP website and the APRA website.

So when Meredith and Cara both, separately even, asked me if I would read their manual and write the foreword for it, I wholeheartedly said yes . . . and give me a deadline.

So, back to my flight. I have about one more hour before touchdown in San Jose. And, yes, that's how wonderfully digestible this manual is! For you, you will want to read through the manual in front of your computer, laptop, tablet, smartphone, etc., and take a look at the information resources Cara and Meredith discuss. This manual should also be kept as a ready reference tool, as you will undoubtedly come across numerous research projects for which you do not recall a specific resource available that meets your current information needs. This manual will help you with those special projects.

For me, this manual took me down memory lane—hiring new researchers, training them, watching them grow. And later on in my career as I moved to share knowledge with numerous nonprofits and educational institutions while working for a for-profit company serving the social sector, I was able to train the development office person, wearing many hats, how to conduct further research utilizing screening results. More memories came flooding back.

I found myself tearing up at one of the true stories in this book. Those of you who know me well or with whom I have chatted via Twitter probably are not surprised by that. I find myself fortunate to be involved with philanthropy, to in some small way contribute to the greater good.

I hope as you further develop your skills and progress in your career, you will see the bigger picture and the lasting effects of your research. This manual is a great place to start!

And may you also one day tear up when you reflect on that great find that led to more people fed this year, more people educated, more children adopted, more animals housed and cared for, safer drinking water, more accessible health care, more discoveries, more good, more good, more good.

Lori Hood Lawson
Self-Proclaimed Data Geek
CEO WorkingPhilanthropy.com
@WorkingLori

Introduction

Welcome to our manual on prospect research. We're going to walk through how nonprofit researchers will search for various types of information about individual donors and prospects. There are many great resources out there, so we thank you for taking this journey with us. From time to time, we'll interject a little conversation into the text to examine areas where it's possible to do things more than one way. There are probably as many ways to research as there are researchers out there, but this manual will look at what information you need in order to do it well.

Even though this is written in a logical, step-by-step fashion, you will probably find yourself working more in circles and loops than step by step. At least that's how we both find ourselves working most of the time. While you will probably have lists and templates available to tell you where to find information, what to look for, and what to do with it, it is just as likely that you will remember to do one thing while you're doing something else and you'll jump back and forth between projects and searches.

You need to have a list or a logical set of steps as you're conducting research to make sure you do everything necessary to address and check all the appropriate resources, even if you end up checking them in a circular fashion. The information in this manual is designed to help you identify what should be in your lists and templates so you can be successful in the field of prospect research and enjoy the work you do to advance nonprofit fundraising.

This manual is divided into four Parts, each dealing with a specific aspect of project research. We decided that the gift pyramid offered a surprisingly appropriate visual aid for examining the levels of research required for different types of prospects.

In chapters 1 through 10, you will learn about the foundations for the profession. This information will lay the groundwork for each of the next sections of chapters.

Chapters 11 through 16 discuss basic research skills for foundational prospects—generally considered annual fund prospects. When presented with a very preliminary request for research, you will probably need the information in this section.

Chapters 17 through 22, Middle of the Road, build upon the first two sections of chapters but can also stand alone. In these chapters, you will learn about research for real estate, gift capacity, and networks. This chapter is the starting point for identifying potential major gift prospects.

Finally, chapters 23 through 27 address the types of research you will conduct when completing a full profile or preparing for a solicitation for a major gift ask.

Although the major topics are segmented in this fashion, we want to make sure you get all the information so you can find what you need regardless of where your prospect falls on the gift pyramid.

Are you ready? Let's start with the foundations! They provide the solid basis you need to have a successful operation.

Part One

Foundations of Prospect Research

In the first ten chapters, we explore the foundations of prospect research. Whatever structure you are trying to build, you likely know that the most fundamental part of the process is establishing the Foundation. We have chosen to start with this part of the pyramid because, without it, you will have a very difficult time conducting any sort of research successfully. Each of these segments is a section in itself, so don't feel like you need to read each chapter beginning to end in order to get the important stuff. Jump around to the chapters that you want to refresh in your mind, or those that you have the opportunity to adjust, or those that you are still learning about in your organization.

We want this manual to be a really useful tool that you can return to time and again to learn something new or to gain a different perspective. While the field of prospect research (and fundraising more generally) is constantly changing, the foundations and tenets remain the same. We all need to have good data that we can locate when we need it and access in an appropriate format to analyze and answer questions for our organization. These foundations are designed to give you the tools to do just that.

4
The
Big
Leagues
•Stocks
•Salary •Company
•Franchises
•Charitable Foundation
•Luxury Items

3 - Middle of the Road

•Real Estate   •Affiliations

•Family   •Interests   •Capacity

2 - Foundational Prospects

•Connections   •Contacts

•Demographics & Public Records

•General Philanthropy & Political Giving

1 - Foundations

•Database   •Templates   •Glossary   •Resources

•Data Mining & Predictive Modeling   •Ethics and Laws

•Pyramids & Ranking   •Bonus Features

Chapter One

Your Database

IN THIS CHAPTER

···→ Questions to ask about your database needs

···→ Choosing an external or internal database

There is a lot of discussion about databases and which are the best for various types of situations or organizations. There are benefits and challenges to whatever you choose, so the best course of action is to review your options and determine which one best addresses the needs of your organization.

A smoothly functioning and secure database is *the* key foundational element of a good organization. It can make or break your success, either by making you a lean, mean, well-organized fundraising machine or by throwing your efforts into total chaos with redundant, confusing, incomplete, or inaccessible prospect information.

Your organization may already have a database that you are using. But if you are considering updating your current database, or changing to a new one, we recommend that you review this section of chapters before you start the process to make sure you are considering all facets of the decision. This is probably the most important tool you have for tracking your prospect information and giving history.

Evaluating Your Database

There are a few vital things to consider concerning your database:

◆ What do you need to put in the database and store?

◆ What do you need to be able to retrieve from the database?

◆ How proficient are your users at locating information?

◆ How much ability do you want to customize how data is stored or accessed?

◆ How much available support do you want, need, and/or have?

To answer these questions, we first must turn our discussion to this single, fundamental one: Internal or External?

Data integrity is a really important concept in this field. And a database that doesn't allow you to find information you need quickly and efficiently makes it much more difficult to keep your data up to date.

important

It can be very helpful to talk to people at organizations similar to yours and investigate what database they are using. Some packaged databases are built for specific types of organizations (e.g., Tessitura is built for arts and cultural organizations, with built-in ticketing functions). New products become available all the time, so this is one great way to research the possibilities.

practical tip

Your organization can choose to purchase a packaged fundraising database, or it is possible to build your own. Let's first take a look at external or packaged databases.

External or Packaged Databases

There are many packaged database options available for purchase, at all price points and time-commitment levels, whether you are a two-person or a two-hundred-person organization. And these packaged databases come with all kinds of built-in features and tools.

Companies that sell such databases include:

◆ Blackbaud Raiser's Edge

◆ Sungard Banner

◆ Datatel Benefactor

◆ Tessitura

◆ Donor2

A packaged database can be a really huge time-saver at reporting time.

practical tip

◆ DonorPerfect

◆ eTapestry

◆ GiftWorks

◆ MatchMaker

◆ PhilanthrAppeal

◆ ResultsPlus

◆ ROI Solutions

◆ Sage

◆ Telosa

◆ open-source versions—there are many, such as ebase, VisibleResults, InfoCentral, CiviCRM, Metrix. Search for open-source tools at techsoup.org.

A limitation of a packaged database is that it is difficult to customize the features and tools yourself. Usually, you must request customization from the company that you purchased from, and that usually means extra costs. And packaged databases can be quite expensive to purchase in the first place.

The advantage of packaged databases is that tools, features, bells, and whistles are ready and waiting for you to use. Just drop your prospect data into it, and it is ready to go. You can pull gift reports, mailing lists, etc., on day one.

With the advent of cloud computing, it is possible for you to purchase a cloud database, where all of your prospect information is stored "in the cloud" or on the server of the company providing the service. In general, "in the cloud" means stored on a computer operated by another party and accessed across the Internet. Cloud storage can present significant cost savings, since your organization does not have to purchase the internal memory or server capacity to store a large amount of data on a large database. It can also present a data security risk, since you are accessing your data via the Internet. Cloud companies should be well aware of such risks, and should be prepared for them, but you need to make sure to completely investigate this aspect of your purchase before making it final.

> Building your own database can be great for facilitating ad hoc reporting.
>
> practical tip

> We have both used both external (packaged) databases and internal (homegrown) databases in our careers, and we believe there really are both benefits and drawbacks to each choice. It depends on the needs and abilities of your organization.
>
> observation

Internal or Homegrown Databases

The benefit of building your database internally is that you can customize it to your heart's delight! You can build all your own tools and reports suited very specifically to your prospect pool, your giving cycle, your institutional background, etc. You can build it on a framework like Access or Sybase at minimal, or definitely lower, cost to your organization (compared with the often significant price tags on packaged databases).

The down side of this approach is that *you* are building the database. First of all, you definitely need to have a staff member (or an entire staff) who is capable of and willing to build a relational database, which is a complicated endeavor. But if you have one or more people who are willing and able, then it can be a wise and cost-effective move for your organization.

Secondly, when building your database, you or your staff will have to figure out all of the aspects and features of the database, the things that are already built into a packaged product. You and your IT staff will have to figure out how to structure the gift reporting, the contact entry, the prospect management system, etc., etc. You may find this quite daunting, or you may be intrigued and excited by the idea of building your own system.

Your organization's database is a choice you should consider very thoughtfully, and we advise you to involve your entire fundraising staff or whole organization in the process of purchasing a packaged product, or changing to a different one, or building your own. You must consider the needs and requirements of everyone on your staff who will use the database as their primary work tool. And don't forget the confidentiality, privacy, and security concerns.

To Recap

◆ Consider all of your database needs and desires before choosing a format.

◆ Assess whether your team has more time or more money available.

◆ Make a database choice that makes sense to you.

Chapter Two

The Tracking Template

IN THIS CHAPTER

- ···→ Why you need a tracking template

- ···→ What your tracking template needs to include

- ···→ Identifying "good to have" sections for your tracking template

Whether your organization has specific metrics for prospect research or not, it is a really good idea to develop and implement a way to track the research requests you receive and complete as well as the projects you carry out on a proactive basis. There are multiple benefits to this method:

- ◆ You can see how much you accomplish.

- ◆ You can demonstrate the causal relationship between your work and significant gifts received by your organizations.

- ◆ You can make the case for more staff or greater resources.

- ◆ You can avoid duplicating research you've already completed or simply keep track of however many prospects you are researching and when the research is needed.

Once you get started tracking, you will probably discover even more benefits than we have mentioned.

Tracking Your Research

One easy tracking document is a simple Excel spreadsheet with columns for who made the request, when the request was made, what is needed, why it's needed, how much time is spent on it each day, the total time spent on the request, and the date it is completed. When using Excel for this purpose, it becomes easy to create a separate worksheet for each fiscal or calendar year to see how much time was spent on various research projects and to compare results from year to year.

In the homegrown database Meredith has at her institution, there is a space on the proposal screen to note specific dates when research was requested and completed. This allows us to quickly pull a report from the database to count how many requests were received and how many were completed in a given time frame. (If it is a proactive research, only a research completed date is entered, which helps distinguish the request types.) This is an easy way to keep a very rudimentary set of metrics that you can compare from year to year.

Other database systems will probably allow you to track your requests and research within the database itself. If you have this functionality, definitely take full advantage of it! Not only will it make your life easier and facilitate "matching" the appropriate research requests with the donors and prospects, but it will remain with your system if you ever leave the organization. New employees can see what information was requested, when it was requested, how long it took to find, and what the results were—all by looking at the prospect research tracking records. This system makes for one less document or paper to keep track of and allows you to more easily pull a report of the research you've completed. Make sure to ask your IT staff, vendor, or customer service representative to explain these tracking mechanisms within your particular system.

Tracking research within the database also will help you manage requests when you have more than one researcher in your organization or when fundraisers want to check on the progress of a research request. This allows you to manage work flow and funnel new requests to the person who will be able to complete them most efficiently based on current workloads.

Essentials for the Tracking Template

At a minimum, your research tracking should include these items, however you choose to track them:

   ◆ request date

   ◆ person making the request

> Try very hard to get a "need by" date when a fundraiser makes a request. A response such as "Whenever you have a chance" will really increase the likelihood that the request gets buried underneath more urgent requests, and then you'll forget about it until the fundraiser calls to ask if you've finished it yet. Most likely, the fundraiser has some sort of time frame in mind when making a request, so remember to find out what the fundraiser is thinking.

important

◆ need-by date

◆ person completing the request

◆ completion date

Bonus Useful Items for Your Tracking Template

If you have the time and ability, it is a good idea to include some of the following items in your tracking files to enable reporting and appropriate time estimates for future endeavors:

◆ type of research requested (simple bio, financial information, capacity, networks, full profile, etc.)

◆ whether the information is needed before the development officer can continue with the relationship (for example, is it necessary to know whether this person has capacity before scheduling the next visit?), as this can help you prioritize requests that are received at similar times

Capacity: Capacity refers to the amount this prospect could feasibly give as a stretch gift (meaning the prospect has to think about it, not just whip out the checkbook) over five years. Generally, capacity gifts go to one of the top-three organizations that a donor supports.

◆ number of hours spent on the request

◆ response from fundraiser about the impact of the research

Regardless of how you choose to do it and the level of granularity you are able to achieve with your tracking systems, make sure you implement something that makes sense in your organization. If you're expected to achieve particular metrics, then those will determine what you track. If your evaluations are more generalized, your tracking can probably take a different format.

To Recap

◆ Track what others ask you to do.

◆ Track what you complete on your own.

◆ Find a tracking mechanism that works for you.

◆ Stick to it.

Chapter Three

The Request Template: What's the Question?

IN THIS CHAPTER

- ···➔ Why you need a request template

- ···➔ What should be included in the request template

In a very general sense, the request template seems like a way to keep your office organized and make sure you get to all the requests that come to you. But there are so many other reasons to make sure your request templates are carefully thought out and implemented. This chapter spends some time focusing on this vital aspect of our profession.

Benefits of a Request Template

Some may bristle when you suggest additional paperwork to fill out when a fundraiser needs to get information from you. Others may try to convince you that a simple phone call (or text, or tweet!) will get enough of the information across for you to get started. We respectfully disagree, and we put forward the following rationale for taking some serious time to look closely at your request template and make it *work* for you.

A well-designed request template helps you:

- ◆ determine what the person making the request *really wants to know*

- ◆ determine what the person making the request *already knows*

- ◆ develop a *framework* and timeline for finding information

The request template, then, helps you identify the REAL question the fundraiser wants you to help answer.

Essential Components of a Request Template

Most of us are guilty of it from time to time, but under most circumstances, you should never reply to a research request without first asking some questions yourself. Those "5W" questions you learned in grade school will come in handy, and you should always try to ask them before you say, "I'll see what I can find." When you design your request template, try to figure out a way to get answers to as many of these questions as you can, right from the outset.

Who?

◆ Who needs the information?

◆ Who is the individual?

◆ Is the individual looking for personal information or corporate information?

◆ Who else is connected to this request?

> The key point here is to help the person making the request think through what's needed. Don't be pushy, but press to help solidify the thinking. It will benefit you both.
>
> important

What?

◆ What does the requester already know?

◆ What is the requester hoping to discover?

◆ What does the requester want you to try to find?

When?

◆ Does the requester have a meeting scheduled already?

◆ Is the requester planning a trip?

◆ Does the requester just want to know if maybe some thought should be given about possibly talking to the prospect in the future?

◆ This year? Next year? Totally unknown?

Where?

◆ Where does the fundraiser want you to look for information (goes back to what the fundraiser wants to know)?

◆ Where did the fundraiser get the information to spark this request?

◆ Where did the fundraiser meet this person?

Why?

◆ Why is this person a good candidate for a visit?

◆ Why are you asking for the information? A meeting? Did someone drop this individual's name? What stage of cultivation or identification is this in? Are you trying to eliminate or include this person in your management list? This question goes back to what the fundraiser want to know and when—another way to get the information you need.

How?

◆ Keep reading to find out.

This depth of questioning may initially seem like overkill when the fundraiser starts with a simple question, and you may get some groans and push-back. However, if you stick to it and the fundraisers learn to expect these kinds of questions every time you conduct research for them, the requests will start to get more refined, you will spend your time more effectively, and fundraisers will get the information they really need, sooner. Everyone wins.

To Recap

◆ Design a *written* format that is required for all requests.

◆ Be diligent in asking follow-up questions from the outset.

◆ Use the template to build a conversation between researchers and frontline fundraisers.

Chapter Four

Profile Templates

IN THIS CHAPTER

···→ Benefits of profile templates

···→ Components of profile types

The profile template, or set of templates, is yet another foundational resource we can create and implement in ways that work for us and our colleagues. Some components are essential, which we will discuss in this chapter, but the formatting is up to you. We'll give you examples, then you can let your creativity go to work designing your own.

Different Templates for Different Purposes

You will want to create several different templates for various types of profiles on individual prospects that you will create in your work and distribute to fundraisers, vice presidents, etc. At the end of each part of chapters in this book, you will see one example of a profile template that includes all of the information discussed up to that point. How you compile the information is not as vital as what information makes sense to include, so we'll address those items briefly here.

Discovery Call Profile

Generally, a fundraiser will not need a significant amount of information before completing an initial discovery profile. So the template for this type might be as simple as a half-sheet of paper printed from your database.

For an initial profile, you need:

❑ Name(s) and ID number if they are in your database already

❑ Contact information (phone, address, email)

❑ Connection to your organization

❑ Donor status or lifetime giving, plus most recent gift amount and date

Event Biography

The event biography may be even shorter than the discovery template. Generally, you will want to create this type of profile if you are inviting many donors or prospective donors to your organization and you want to highlight their specific interests for the executives in your organization so the conversation can flow easily. There won't be much time or ability to memorize long bits of text about each person, but a paragraph or a few bullet points will go a long way toward making people feel comfortable and important at your event.

For a brief event biography that an executive needs, you may even need fewer items:

❑ Name(s)

❑ Donor status (e.g., major donor, annual fund donor, lifetime member)

❑ Snapshot of a couple of talking points (e.g., interests, occupation)

Complete Profile Prior to Solicitation

In times past, the full profile from a prospect research office could be ten to twenty pages of text about the prospective donor. You can imagine the blood, sweat, and tears that went into some of those! These days, we no longer tend to create long tomes, but that doesn't mean we don't pass forward all the vital pieces of information about prospects.

For a full profile, you need just about all of the pieces we mention in this manual:

❑ Name(s)

❑ Contact information

❑ Connections to your organization

❑ Employment information

❑ Giving summary to your organization

❑ General philanthropy and political giving summary

❏ Interests, shared networks

❏ General wealth or net worth

❏ Real estate holdings

❏ Other luxury items owned or collections held

❏ Estimated major gift capacity

❏ Estimated likelihood or propensity to give

Sometimes you need something in between. We will give you some ideas within these pages, but we encourage you to engage your coworkers to define the profile templates that work for your organization and that give everyone the needed information in a way that makes sense.

To Recap

◆ Design a set of profile templates to fit the needs of your organization.

◆ Don't redo the kitchen if someone just asked for a clean plate.

Chapter Five

Definitions and a Glossary

IN THIS CHAPTER

- ···→ Why you need a glossary

- ···→ Deciding what to put in your glossary

- ···→ Planning revisions to your glossary

You're thinking, "What, they have an entire *chapter* on the glossary and definitions?!" And we respond, "Yes!" Because agreeing on terms and concepts with your coworkers is absolutely vital to your mutual success.

Recommendations

This chapter might seem a bit odd at the outset, since we will won't really give you as many definitions as you might expect in a glossary. Nevertheless, keep reading. We have a lot of really important information to cover, and how well you follow these guidelines can have a pretty significant impact on how easy or difficult your job becomes.

Recommendation 1: Compile a Glossary

So, our first recommendation here is to actually devise a set of common definitions and glossary for your organization. Perhaps there is one already in place, but we're guessing there are a few things that would benefit from clarification, even in the most well-established shops.

Recommendation 2: Revisit the Glossary

Second, and equally important, get your team together regularly to revisit the definitions you created and to make sure they still fit your goals, policies, and procedures. Hopefully, you won't end up changing many of them during this process, but it's very good to remind everyone from time to time (annually would be good) what you all agree you mean by certain words and how that affects your mutual work.

Also, you might want to consider adding a glossary revisitation to the standard operating procedures when a new staff member arrives. Instead of just distributing the terms and definitions along with the tomes of other information a new employee receives, use the opportunity to get together and discuss the words and concepts. This helps solidify the ideas in people's minds and also allows everyone to be present in case discussions and questions arise.

Recommendation 3: Expand the Glossary

Third, you want to make sure that your glossary is sort of a living document that expands when you need to clarify terms or concepts within your organization. A good rule of thumb might be that if more than two people ask you about the same type of idea, then it's time to get the group together and decide what that topic means to your organization and then officially add it to your glossary.

Recommendation 4: Terms to Include

You thought we were never going to get to a list of what this glossary should include, didn't you? Well, have no fear! Here are some common terms in fundraising that can have different definitions based on your organizational characteristics.

◆ Major Gift ($5,000? $50,000? $100,000? Some other amount?)

◆ Prospect Cultivation Meeting

◆ Prospect Cultivation Strategy

◆ Gift

◆ Prospect Visit (There are many names for meeting with a prospect that fall under this term, but mainly what you want to define is "what is a significant visit?" Or what "counts" as a prospect visit for your fundraisers metrics? Is it simply saying hello at the annual auction? Or should it include discussion of

> Define "gift?" Yes, really! When you speak in general terms about people's giving, do you most often want to know about pledges they have made (what about write-offs or matching gifts?) or actual cash in the door? What about gifts-in-kind? You might want to know all of these things, but try to settle on different definitions, if possible, to alleviate any confusion.

important

interests and the gift? Most organizations qualify different kinds of visits for tracking and metrics purposes.)

◆ Contact Report (This one is really important and actually factors into your work as a researcher in a significant way.)

◆ Prospect Manager (Is this the fundraiser responsible for soliciting a gift? What if there are a few employees working together on the proposal? What does this person need to do to "manage" the prospect relationship? Is this the person who helps the fundraisers develop a strategy?)

◆ Prospect Assignment (When is someone assigned? When you begin discovery? When you've done due diligence and research and determined that someone is a good prospect for a major gift? If someone is assigned, does that mean no one else can talk to that prospect or just that the assigned manager should be given a heads up first?)

◆ Research Options. We'll discuss this in much more depth in the next section of chapters, but it helps to go over these choices briefly with your whole staff so you all know what is meant by an initial research request, a full profile, a financial capacity rating, and everything in between. This will streamline the process by helping everyone know what to ask for and what kinds of information they can expect to receive. This will also help to convey how long you as the researcher will spend on various projects. You could even define it as "The ten-minute research option gives you these three things," "The two-hour research option gives you these things," and "The full-day research option gives you this."

If a contact report says, "Had a great lunch with Tim on Friday," you're not going to have a lot of information to go on.

But what if the contact report says, "Met Tim for lunch on Friday. He discussed a number of projects he's interested in, including the new science lab facilities and the library collections for biological sciences. He wants to meet again next month to talk about how he's helped some other institutions move forward with gifts like these."

Now you know that (a) Tim is really invested in biological sciences, (b) Tim probably has some financial capacity for major gifts, (c) Tim has a strong affinity to your institution and wants to be involved in what's going on and even mentioned when he wants to meet again, and (d) you need to do some follow-up research on capacity, interests, and other projects he's been involved with before this fundraiser meets with Tim next month.

Example

There are certainly other terms and ideas that will come up in your organization that warrant a full-group discussion so that everyone stays on the same page. That's why we included recommendations two and three above. By consistently revisiting and expanding together your list of definitions, you will all stay closer to having the same understanding of what fundraising research means at your organization.

To Recap

◆ Familiar terms don't always mean the same thing to everyone—discuss them together.

◆ Continue your dialog about definitions, frequently

Chapter Six

Resources: Finding the Best for You

IN THIS CHAPTER

    ···➔ Components of a fully stocked tool kit

    ···➔ The Authors' Favorites

    ···➔ Compiling your own resource library

There are many great resources out there for our work in prospect research and the field of development fundraising—and the list grows as we speak. In this chapter, we hope to identify a few of the main resources and then give you the questions you should ask when you're trying to determine which route to go when acquiring resources for your work.

Essential Components of a Fully Stocked Tool Kit

Every researcher will undoubtedly have a personal set of favorite resources to return to, again and again. We will definitely share some of ours with you in these pages, but we also want to draw your attention to the major components of the resource tool kit, so you can figure out what specifically fits your needs from within that framework.

You probably want to compile your own resource library consisting of

    ◆ Books

    ◆ Websites

    ◆ Online search tools and databases

    ◆ Reports and publications

- ◆ List serves

- ◆ Professional associations

- ◆ People networks

You'll notice over time that there are a few key resources in each of these sections that continually show up on everyone's lists. But there is also a lot of room for choosing your own. And especially with online resources, the choices are continually expanding, so make sure you stay on top of what's most current.

Meredith's Top Ten Favorite Resources

1. iWave Prospect Research Online (PRO)

2. PRSPCT-L and FUNDSVCS listserves

3. Manta

4. Wealth Engine

5. Accurint (Alumni Finder)

6. Target Analytics—Research Point

7. Google

8. Securities and Exchange Commission (sec.gov)—really helpful for corporate research

9. Zillow

10. Friends and colleagues I have met through the listserves

> I have an eleventh, so that I can mention that NOZA, Guidestar, ZoomInfo, High Net Worth, TrackWealth, HEP GiftsPlus Matching Gifts, LexisNexis Real Estate, and several other really great resources are part of the ten listed above, which is why they are not listed separately.
>
>

Cara's Top Ten Favorite Resources

1. LexisNexis for Development Professional (expensive, but so worth it)

2. iWave Prospect Research Online (PRO)

3. pulawski.net

4. Zillow

5. Blackbaud's ResearchPoint and Target Analytics wealth screening (dependent upon the number of records, so can be reasonably affordable and can be followed by a la carte services)

6. Google

7. PRSPCT-L

8. supportingadvancement.com (great resource for forms and such)

9. superpages.com

10. Friends and colleagues at other institutions

You'll see more of our favorite resources in the next three major chapter sections as we discuss how to conduct research for various types of projects.

Selecting Your Resources

To some extent, the resources you need depend on the specifics of your job and the needs of your organization. As you will see in the remainder of this manual, different types of prospects look different from each other and require different sources to conduct the research.

If you're in a smaller shop or are focused primarily on the annual fund, then you need a different set of resources from someone whose sole job consists of capacity ratings for super-high-level executives. We arranged this book so that if you're going to be researching a specific type of prospect, you will find in one place the suggestions for compiling those resources.

As far as resources go, it's also a good idea to periodically check out the books, articles, and listserves that frontline fundraisers read. This helps keep you on the same page as those you are collaborating with and helps you understand more about their jobs and how the information you find can be most useful to their success. You will probably also want to cultivate relationships with fundraisers outside of your organization who can serve as sounding boards and resources for you. Many of the resources we use are listed in the appendix, and we encourage you to refer to those often when you encounter new situations.

To make your resource tool kit make more sense, we provide the following checklist:

❑ Identify three to five primary needs of your organization.

❑ Determine how much money you have available for resources.

❑ Determine how much time you have available to research.

❑ Cross-list the resources with your needs, funds, and time.

❑ Do some trial runs with subscription resources.

❑ Make a few key choices for resources.

❑ Evaluate whether your needs are being met or whether you should consider other options.

 to-do lists

To Recap

◆ Choosing good resources is fundamental to success.

◆ Creating your own tool kit of favorites is easy (and fun!).

Chapter Seven

Data Mining and Predictive Modeling

IN THIS CHAPTER

···◆ What Is Data Mining?

···◆ What Is Predictive Modeling?

We're just going to touch on data mining and predictive modeling here, because we really felt that those topics deserve their own manual (stay tuned for a future publication) that deals specifically with the nuances of those tasks and that they are different enough from "research" to allow for just a passing glance here.

Data Mining

When you speak of data mining, you are often looking into your own database files and pulling out information to see what you have. Some potential questions that data mining might answer:

◆ Do you have a number of donors who have been giving consistently each consecutive year that you didn't know about before?

◆ How is the class of 1965 giving in compared with the class of 1985? What characteristics are different that might account for those giving differences?

You can do some initial mining on your own, using spreadsheets or something similar. You will probably have good luck mining data using Excel, Rapid Insight Advizor, Wealth Engine, or Crystal Reports.

Joshua Birkholz from Benz Whaley Flessner is very knowledgeable about data analytics, and his book *Fundraising Analytics* is definitely one you should check out when you want to mine data

Data Mining: either an informal or formal process of finding what information or which prospects are in your database. It might be as simple as pulling a list of everyone who satisfies XYZ criteria, or it might be a complicated series of steps involving residential location, giving history, interests, and capacity data, for example.

on your own. Peter Wylie's *Data Mining for Fundraisers* is another great book to teach you about this topic. You should also try to attend any conference sessions led by either of these guys—they know their stuff!

Predictive Modeling

Predictive modeling is a bit different and a bit more challenging. When you're creating a model, you basically determine the characteristics of your target donors (based on your past major donors) and then see who else in your database has those characteristics but is not yet a donor. You can do some pretty basic modeling without a lot of statistics or analytical background, but you will probably have more success if you use some of these tools for modeling: Rapid Insight Advizor, DataDesk, Wealth Engine, Blackbaud/Target Analytics, SPSS or SAS. Again, the books by Josh Birkholz (*Fundraising Analytics*) and Peter Wylie (*Data Mining for Fundraisers*) will be great resources for you in this endeavor.

This was indeed a short chapter! These are very important aspects of fundraising research, but they also go into significantly more depth than the scope of this manual. Most readers are likely doing individual prospect research and not spending much of their time doing data mining or predictive modeling at this point. So we wanted to mention these ideas here, briefly, and then ensure that we can devote ample time and space to them in another manual.

Predictive Modeling: process of looking at a particular set of donors in your database and creating an algorithm that describes them, and then applying that algorithm to other potential donors in your database to see who "looks" the same and has a high likelihood of being a future donor.

To Recap

◆ Data Mining is conducted when you pull information you already have out of your database.

◆ Predictive Modeling uses characteristics of your current donors to suggest potential new ones.

◆ These concepts are really fun to explore. Don't be afraid of the math requirements. You can do it!

Chapter Eight

Ethics and Laws

IN THIS CHAPTER

··→ Why Ethics Matter

··→ Where to Find Ethics Statements

In this field, you are dealing with really personal information. So it is important to remember and to remind people frequently that we as researchers are held to a high level of accountability when it comes to the ethical gathering and use of data.

Why it Matters

By this point in your prospect research career (even if today is your first day), you've realized that you are privy to a *lot* of information about people. Now most of this information is public, and we use only publicly available sources to retrieve it. But there is still a lot available to us. And when we combine it all in one place, in a donor profile or in our organization's database, it becomes a very clear picture of the prospect. So we need to be cautious and treat that picture (the prospect and donor) with respect.

Ethics matter because:

◆ We have access to a *lot* of sensitive data.

◆ We are called to be responsible stewards of data we find.

◆ We are representatives of our organizations.

◆ All people deserve to be treated respectfully regardless of the information we find.

◆ We want to protect our good name and continue to make a good name for others in our profession.

Starting from Within: Internal Confidentiality Agreement

When thinking about ethics, it's fair to say that you should start at "home." That is to say, meet with your colleagues and other individuals who work at your organization and discuss how ethics applies to your mutual work.

In larger organizations, it is likely that you already have some kind of confidentiality statement in place. For smaller organizations that do not have such an agreement in place, it is *highly* advisable that you get one and have all employees sign it. You are legally responsible for the data you collect, keep, and manage. If that data gets stolen or leaked, you could be in a lot of legal trouble.

You can find confidentiality agreement templates on the Internet or in other books and manuals. We recommend that you get one if you don't have one already.

Where to Find Ethics Statements of Our Profession

One good tip is to frame and display the Donor Bill of Rights and the APRA Code of Ethics in your office so they are visible to everyone who enters and so you have it in your mind at all times. We have reprinted these two documents, along with the Codes of Ethics for AFP and AASP, which also address this field, in the appendix. When it comes to ethics, the basic foundation to remember is that if you would feel uncomfortable with someone knowing something about you, you probably don't want to gather it about others.

> Sometimes it is necessary for you to uncover and learn very sensitive information about prospects and donors. But before you encounter that situation, make sure there's a policy for what to do with what you find.
>
> For example, you might need to check whether a prospective donor is involved in some legal or ethical problems before approaching her for a naming gift on a building. You probably will not want to enter all of that research in your database, but you can allude to it or call the fundraiser and say, "The charges did exist, but they've been dropped." And then you move on. When in doubt, check with your legal counsel.
>
> **Example**

To Recap

◆ It is of the utmost importance to act ethically in this profession.

◆ If your organization doesn't have a confidentiality policy, create one and have everyone sign it.

◆ Follow the Ethics Statements of Our Profession, which are reprinted in the appendix for reference.

Chapter Nine

Campaign Pyramid and Capacity Rank Categories

IN THIS CHAPTER

···→ Creating a campaign pyramid

···→ Assigning prospects to pyramid levels

G oing into a fundraising campaign of any sort, most organizations put together a "pyramid" to help determine the levels of giving and the number of gifts and/or prospects needed at each level to enable them to reach the total fundraising goal. It is a good visual tool to help keep you on track as you move through your campaign time period.

The Campaign Pyramid

A diagram of gift levels in fundraising is generally called a campaign pyramid. Whether your diagram actually resembles a pyramid or looks more like the Seattle Space Needle or some sort of abstract shape not identifiable in geometry, for the purposes of this discussion, it will be called the "pyramid." Your Foundational Prospects (chapters 11 through 16) are the bottom layer of the pyramid, made up of many small gifts from a lot of people. Your middle-of-the-road prospects (chapters 17 through 22) are asked for slightly larger amounts and are made up of a smaller number of actual asks. And the top of your pyramid, the Big Leagues (chapters 23 through 27) generally consist of a very few donors who give the largest proportion of your total dollars raised.

> Campaign Pyramid: A pictorial story of how you are going to reach your fundraising goal. Each major donor fits into one place on the pyramid correlating to the size of gift you anticipate. In many cases these days, the pyramid is shaped more like the Space Needle, with more large gifts coming from fewer donors.
>
> definition

Here is one way to calculate a campaign pyramid, from the consulting firm of Alexander McNabb & Co. in Chicago, Illinois (alexandermacnab.com/CapGiftCamp/2Calculator2.htm):

Gifts	Gift Range Level	Percentage of Goal	Number of Prospects
1	10%–20% of goal	10%–20%	4–5
2	5%–10% of goal	15%	6–8
4	2.5% of goal	10%	16
8	1% of goal	10%	30
16	0.6% of goal	10%	50
32	0.3% of goal	10%	100
64	0.15% of goal	10%	200
Many		5%–15%	Huge

So, this is not actually a pyramid, but it explains for you how many prospects you need at each level to achieve any goal and/or how to break up your goal into pieces so that you can have numbers to aim for as you work through your campaign.

Of course, you can conduct a campaign without this kind of chart. But why would you want to? It's not like eating a large piece of pie—one bite at a time. Campaigns are complicated, multilayered endeavors. If you have a sizable campaign goal and you need multiple donors to achieve it, you will best accomplish your goal by setting markers for yourself and for anyone working on the campaign so that you know you are making progress toward your goal within a reasonable amount of time.

Campaign pyramids break the whole process down for you, so you can go bite by bite in each level. They also make it very easy for you to track your progress.

observation

This pyramid chart, from consultant Marc A. Pitman at about.com, is a completed example of a campaign pyramid for a goal of $1,000,000 (nonprofit.about.com/od/fundraising/ss/How-To-Build-A-Gift-Chart-For-A-Fundraising-Campaign.htm):

Gift Amount	Number of Gifts	Number of Prospects	Cumulative Total
$150,000	1	4	$150,000
$75,000	2	8	$300,000
$40,000	4	16	$460,000
$20,000	8	24	$620,000
$10,000	16	32	$780,000
$5,000	24	48	$900,000
$2,500	40	80	$1,000,000

You can turn these charts into actual pyramids if you have the skills. For example:

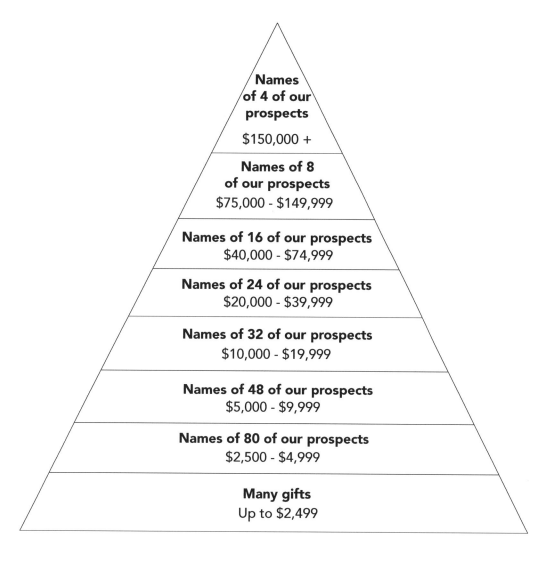

Names of 4 of our prospects
$150,000 +

Names of 8 of our prospects
$75,000 - $149,999

Names of 16 of our prospects
$40,000 - $74,999

Names of 24 of our prospects
$20,000 - $39,999

Names of 32 of our prospects
$10,000 - $19,999

Names of 48 of our prospects
$5,000 - $9,999

Names of 80 of our prospects
$2,500 - $4,999

Many gifts
Up to $2,499

This is one of those invaluable organizing tools that will help you stay on track for all the months or years of your campaign and allow you to present your progress to your executives and/or your board. We cannot recommend it enough, no matter how big or small you are!

Find a wall space in your office where you can have a physical diagram of the pyramid with donor and prospect names. One idea might be to have each gift level represented by a different color of paper so that you can see where you anticipated a donor would give and where the donor actually gave. Graphical representation of the pyramid will really help make it a useful, living document to guide fundraising activities in your organization. When the gifts close, put a sticker or check mark on those places in the pyramid, or cover up the whole space with a piece of black paper to give you a visual of your progress toward the goal.

Team Activity

A really great activity for your team when you're compiling the campaign pyramid is to add actual names to each space on the chart. In the above example, for a $1 million campaign, you need four prospects for your top level, so you should have names of four individuals or couples you know who have the *capacity* and *likelihood* to give you a gift at the level of $150,000 or above. For the second level, identify the actual names of eight prospects who have the capacity and affinity to give you a gift at $75,000 or above. You don't want to put prospects in more than one level, but do keep in mind that there's a good chance that people who don't give at the higher levels where you originally placed them will give at one of the other levels on your pyramid.

As a researcher, you'll be busy identifying the prospects for these sections of the pyramid. You may find many examples of pyramid tracking charts that help you see what your organization already knows and how many prospects you have at each level. This information helps determine (at the outset) how many additional prospects you need to identify and cultivate for each of the levels to help your organization move toward success.

To Recap

◆ Campaign pyramids are very useful tools.

◆ Assign *real names* to each space on your pyramid.

◆ Use research on capacity to move prospects around if necessary.

Chapter Ten

Bonus Features

IN THIS CHAPTER

···→ Going through the daily motions

···→ Trading tips among friends

···→ Choosing your own favorites

A Day in the Life

This chapter recounts a literal day that occurred recently. We thought it would be fun to include it as a chapter here.

Arrival at work—

Make a pot of coffee/cup of tea.

8:00–8:20 a.m.—Read e-newsletters.

8:20–8:40 a.m.—Read news alerts that I've set up through Google, Prospect Research Online, Meltwater News, Crain's Chicago Business, and Accurint. Update information in the database or print profiles that need to be added to the database. (Depending on how long it will take to do the updates—if it's quick, enter it now; if it's lengthy, print it for later.)

8:40–9:00 a.m.—Get email from fundraiser asking to have a prospect removed from top prospects listing. Meet briefly with coworker to verify the process we are using to show prospects as "closed" rather than "removed from assignment." Then update the record and reply to the fundraiser with the steps in the process so that the fundraiser can complete the steps in future situations.

9:00–10:45 a.m.—Continue with search for philanthropy for a company I began researching yesterday. The gifts and sponsorships do not show up under "charitable giving" in any of the paid searches, so I look online for annual report mentions. The fundraiser who made this request is looking specifically for information about whether the company will donate gifts-in-kind or give discounts on their product that we need.

10:45–11:00 a.m.—Email, mailbox, etc., break.

11:00–11:30 a.m.—Continue with Google search for company giving.

11:30 a.m.–noon—Listservs, newsletters, other emails. (Important e-newsletters include Philanthropy News Digest, Crain's, University Business, Inside Higher Ed, Academic Impressions, CoolData blog, and Jason's Blog: The Far Edge of Promise.)

Noon–12:30 p.m.—Lunch!

12:30–1:00 p.m.—Begin writing up summary of research. Run a quick report in Crystal Reports for anyone whose Business Name is like the company name, and find ten individuals. Print profiles to add to research information.

> It's always a good idea to take advantage of the webinars offered by the vendors; they give you insights into using the products fully, help you understand the differences between the various products, and also just give you some good tips!
>
>  practical tip

1:00–2:00 p.m.—Vendor webinar for Research Point

2:00–2:45 p.m.—Assorted office projects, talking with coworkers about projects, etc.

2:45–4:00 p.m.—Continue with write-up of research results and send to Development Officer.

Helpful Tips

◆ *Always* use more than one source for information when conducting Internet research. The Internet is rife with outdated or incorrect information. Have two sources at minimum and three if you can manage it.

◆ Look for resources that will help you understand aspects of the research field that you might not know a lot about. At a recent used-book sale at the library, I found a copy of "Farm and Ranch Financial Records," which has a lot of vital information about how farmers and ranchers fill out financial statements, tax forms, etc., and can help me with valuing farm and ranch property, since there are a number of people around my area who fit into that category.

◆ Make sure your resources also contain the contact information of a few key colleagues who are familiar with prospect research. In some cases, it's helpful if they work in the same industry as you so that they can help you understand the specific situations you encounter. In other cases, it is useful if the colleagues work in a different industry that might have totally different situations that are "everyday" to them and perhaps new to you.

◆ Join several listserves about the field: PRSPCT-L, FUNDSVCS, ADVANCE-L, PROSPECT-DMM are all really great for quickly getting in touch with people who can give you tips and ideas for your work. The archives for several of these lists are also treasure troves of information for you to mine.

◆ If a manual for prospect research specific to your organization doesn't already exist, create something that will compile all of your processes together in one place, making it easy to figure out where you are in a project—just in case you get distracted by something else—and will provide an easy way to explain to others what it is you do.

◆ Join a few professional organizations. APRA is a great one devoted specifically to prospect researchers. AASP is for advancement services professionals, which involves a growing component of researchers. CASE is great for education institutions. CharityChannel is great for individuals in all aspects of the fundraising profession. AHP, the Association for Healthcare Philanthropy, is designed specifically for that industry.

◆ Find a handful of blogs to keep track of from time to time. Some of our favorites include:

   ◆ The High Edge of Promise (jasonmcneal.com)

   ◆ CoolData (cooldata.wordpress.com)

   ◆ Penelope Burk, Burk's Blog (burksblog.com)

   ◆ Blackbaud's Prospect Research Blog (prospectresearch.com)

   ◆ Donor Scape's Blog (donorscape.com/blog)

(There are surely many others out there. Please join the conversation in the Prospect Research group at CharityChannel.com and share your thoughts and other great blogs you follow!)

Resource Wrap-Up

Spend a few minutes before you move on in this manual to catalog your own research resource library. Go ahead. We'll even give you space to write it in right here:

◆ Five books I need in my library:

_____

_____

_____

_____

_____

◆ Ten web resources I need in my bookmarks:

◆ Biographical

_____

_____

◆ Occupation/Employment

_____

_____

◆ Assets/Real Estate

_____

_____

◆ Other Heading: _____

_____

_____

_____

_____

◆ Subscription services I need to examine:

_____

_____

_____

_____

◆ People I need to keep in touch with regularly:

Name	Email	Phone

To Recap

◆ Break up the day in manageable sections of varied but productive activities.

◆ Do break for lunch.

◆ Summarize in writing what you've learned while it is fresh.

◆ Make time for professional development.

Part Two

Foundational Prospects

In chapters 11 through 16, we explore Foundational Prospects. As the name implies, Foundational Prospects are the bases upon which your fundraising program rests. These are often referred to as "annual fund" prospects or similar names that suggest you return to these donors year after year to provide small but sustaining gifts. In arts organizations or public radio, and other organizations of that nature, these donors are often referred to as "members" who continually demonstrate commitment to help meet the organization's financial needs. Typically, Foundational Prospects are asked for smaller amounts of money (than major gift or planned gift prospects), often at levels up to $1,000 each year.

We'll look at how you would conduct research on these Foundational Prospects. Generally, you will research information like basic connections to your organization, contact information, demographic data, and basic summaries of the prospect's philanthropy and political giving. Research for these prospects helps you get a better picture of who they are and whether they would be interested in giving to your organization. Many times, you will conduct this research for larger groups at a time as part of segmenting your database for an annual appeal. We've broken out each of the main research topics into a separate chapter, so let's get started.

4
The
Big
Leagues
•Stocks
•Salary •Company
•Franchises
•Charitable Foundation
•Luxury Items

3 - Middle of the Road

•Real Estate   •Affiliations

•Family   •Interests   •Capacity

2 - Foundational Prospects
•Connections   •Contacts
•Demographics & Public Records
•General Philanthropy & Political Giving

1 - Foundations
•Database   •Templates   •Glossary   •Resources
•Data Mining & Predictive Modeling   •Ethics and Laws
•Pyramids & Ranking   •Bonus Features

Chapter Eleven

Connection to Your Organization

IN THIS CHAPTER

···→ Finding connections

···→ Linking connections that already exist

···→ Leveraging connections

The connection that prospects and donors have to your organization is perhaps *the* most fundamental topic we will discuss in this manual. If you don't know how they're connected, how will you leverage that connection to find the best programs for them to support? Remember that in fundraising, it is our job (all of us, not just the frontline fundraisers) to help facilitate the types of gifts that donors want to make. We help determine the right ask amount, for the right project, and the right time, as well as the right person to make the ask. And all of these "rights" hinge on a connection to us, the researchers.

Looking Within

Hopefully this information is already available to you in your database. If not, do whatever you need to do to get a place to add it to your database. Because once you find it, you don't really want to have to go looking for it again in a year or two.

And if the prospect has an opportunity to have more than one connection to your organization, it's a good idea to identify all of those connections and prioritize them so that the right person builds the relationship with the prospect. That is to say, if you're a college or university, maybe that relationship builder can be an alumnus, a parent, and a board member all at the same time. Knowing all of these things will ensure your institution makes the appropriate decisions about who will solicit that individual. Depending on your institutional characteristics, the

---

Research Your Rights!

◆ The right person

◆ The right ask amount

◆ The right time

◆ The right purpose

principle

---

annual fund director or a student might make perfect sense, and in other circumstances, it will be best if the president, vice president, or someone else from the board makes the connection.

Finding New Connections

If *the* prospect's connection to you is not already in the database, fear not. Here are a few tips to get you started in uncovering these important connections.

◆ Conduct an alumni/constituent/friend survey and let the prospect tell you.

◆ Search your database for the prospect's relatives or friends to see if you have a notation of that connection (maybe you have a son's alumni record in your database, so you can determine that your prospect is a parent, or maybe the spouse or sibling is an artist who has donated works to your annual art auction).

◆ Look into the prospect's giving history at your organization and see if you get any clues by what in particular the prospect chooses to support.

◆ Ask around at your organization to learn who knows the prospect. Much like the six-degrees-of-separation activity, surely you will be able to find the true connection if you ask around. If you're asked to research someone who is new to you, then ask the requester how they know the person or who provided the name, and then ask that person. Networking is a vital aspect of the fundraising field, and it's a good idea to utilize it here as well.

> If there is *any* possibility that a prospect can have more than one connection to your organization, make sure you have options for all of those possibilities and an internal hierarchy for how they will be displayed or used. It will save a lot of time and frustration in the long run.
>
>

Utilizing Connections to Research Foundational Prospects

Once you've found a connection to the organization, you can start to follow up on the requests you receive based on those connections.

For Foundational Prospects, a request here might look something like this:

◆ Can you find me the names of everyone who has ever attended one of our "Save the Koala" events since 1975?

◆ I need to contact all business school alumni from the classes of 1994 through 1999 to request help setting up this new scholarship.

◆ Let's make a list of all the "grateful patients" from the last year to invite them to our open house/meet the doctors event.

◆ We're having a fundraising dinner for the new Picasso exhibit. Can you find me some prospective attendees?

◆ I'd like to invite all former athletes in the Tucson area to the upcoming football game we will play there.

In each of these instances, you are mining your database for lists of prospects based on their *connection* to your organization.

This is a fundamental step, and you will probably be asked for requests like this often. These are often not in-depth requests for research *about* these people, just a list of who fits the qualifications. You may, however, need to conduct further in-depth research about *some* of the prospects in the future as the fundraiser gets closer to soliciting for the specific project. So it's good to keep that in mind.

To Recap

◆ Remember to look for connections in your database first.

◆ Track all connections a donor has to your organization.

◆ Use all available sources to explore new connections.

Chapter Twelve

Contact Information

IN THIS CHAPTER

--→ Batch Update Services

--→ Individual Look-Ups

Current contact information might be the first thing you should tackle when you start a research project for Foundational Prospects—or any other prospects for that matter. You need to know where they live and have a correct way to get in touch with them. In fact, you might even need to do this before you can find a person's connections to your organization. So if you couldn't find the connections in the last chapter, read through this one, find the correct contact information, and then go back to the connections and look again. You might be surprised at what you're able to find the second time around with a little more data to go on.

Where Contact Information Lives

NCOA (National Change of Address service from the US Postal Service) is a great resource to accomplish this en masse if you are planning a mailing or phone calls to a large number of people at once.

Make sure your development officer doesn't already know this information before you go looking for it! Don't assume that what's in your database is the same as what the fundraiser knows to be true—it would be great if your data is that current, but don't assume that it is.

If you are trying to research contact information for a handful of prospects or just one at a time, then it makes sense to look them up through an online search engine like Whitepages or Superpages if you're looking for a free site.

> I always check my contact information in a couple of different sources to make sure that I am getting the most accurate information. But you need to be a bit careful with this, because several sources might get their information from the same original source (e.g., LexisNexis and Accurint are the same company/source with different names. And other companies rely on LexisNexis for address and real estate data). That is to say, make sure your "different sources" aren't just the same information packaged by different companies.
>
> **watch out!**

If you have a few fee-based sources, sites like Accurint, LexisNexis for Development Professionals, ResearchPoint, or Wealth Engine can help you find not only the current contact information but also some historical contact information (past addresses, etc., to match with your records perhaps?) and names of relatives.

Accurint can be especially helpful here because you can use it to search for someone with the address that you have, and it will find everyone who has lived at that address. If your prospect is no longer living there, it will most likely give you the most current address and phone number.

In Wealth Engine, you will get an indicator called "historical record" if the property is not where the prospects currently live. So even if you don't get a new address, you will know to look for one because yours is out of date.

We've just mentioned a few of the subscription services here. There are many! And we find that the majority have the same levels of reliability, so in this case, it makes sense to use the source you trust most or the one(s) you have purchased for other reasons.

Important Update Questions to Consider

As the researcher, you will likely encounter a lot of prospect contact information that doesn't match what you have in your database. There can be multiple reasons for this—some of them even good. But it's essential, nonetheless, to consider questions about the data you already have and the data you discover when they don't match. Good questions to ask yourself include:

◆ Is this an additional property or business listing?

◆ Is this an outdated property or business listing?

◆ Is this the current property or business listing?

If you can't figure it out from the records you have, try a few other sources, and then give all the information to the fundraiser who can verify correct information during a prospect visit.

Another important step in keeping contact information current is identifying who makes changes to the information you have and when. Find your organization's policy on record updates and review it to make sure it makes sense. To help facilitate that discussion, have an objective conversation about some of these questions:

◆ Who is supposed to be tracking changes and updating contact information?

◆ How many people have access to it?

◆ How many people should have access to it?

◆ What tracking mechanisms are in place for ensuring accuracy?

If you have too many people updating the same fields of information, it will be pretty easy for them to inadvertently change things that were just changed, and then your data gets all cloudy again. Best to have just a handful of people who make updates, and if others come across new information, they should send it to those people.

Too many moving parts make it really, really difficult to maintain data integrity.

Batch Updates

Several resources for contact information as a batch process are included here. As with most resources, specifics of your organization have much impact on what constitutes the "best" choice, so you should talk with vendors about your needs and their options.

◆ AlumniFinder

◆ Relevate Group, formerly Telematch (primarily phone append)

◆ Pacific East Research (primarily phone append)

◆ Blackbaud Data Enrichment Services

◆ Harris Connect

◆ HEP Development Services

◆ Brian Lacy (brianlacy.com)

Locating current contact information generally takes just a few minutes. It's an especially important undertaking if you are trying to re-engage prospects that your organization hasn't contacted recently.

To Recap

◆ Never *assume* your database is the most current information (but hats off to you if you *know* it is!).

◆ Ask questions when data you find doesn't match your records.

◆ Cross-reference your contact records for verification.

Chapter Thirteen

Demographics, Vital Statistics, and Public Records

IN THIS CHAPTER

···→ Useful demographics for fundraising

···→ Finding demographic information

emographics are the basic bits of information that tell you who your prospect is. They can either be really quick to find or take loads of time. Wherever possible, it helps to store these in your database so you can query people based on particular sets of demographics (also known as data mining). This chapter will discuss which characteristics are most important and how to go about finding them.

Demographic Factors to Consider

An interesting concept about demographics is that they are really vital for batching prospects together with others like them, but they constantly change, so you can't just find them once, rest on your laurels, and move on.

Demographics that are helpful in this line of work:

◆ gender

◆ age or age range

◆ marital status

◆ occupation

◆ family status (children? in what stage of life?)

Demographics for One Prospect at a Time

There are multiple avenues to explore demographic variables for prospects on an individual basis.

- ◆ Many of the paid services, such as Accurint, Wealth Engine, Target Analytics/Research Point, LexisNexis for Development Professionals, etc., will give you access to a number of these pieces of data when you look up a complete profile.

- ◆ You can also find or infer many through public sides of social networking sites and other Internet resources.

- ◆ If you're prospecting for a school, you can look through old yearbooks to find indications of age range, gender, athletic participation, and other activities, and then add that information to your database.

> Adding demographic data to your database from old yearbooks or annual reports and material such as that can be a great project for a student worker during the summer or for an intern who has small pieces of "down time" and can just pick up the project when time allows.
>
> practical tip

- ◆ You can go to the county courthouse and look at public records for births, deaths, marriages, and divorces.

- ◆ You can search online databases through a public or university library for records of birth, death, marriage, divorce, and employment announcements.

- ◆ You can simply read the local newspaper(s) for your area or the areas where you have large concentrations of donors to look for updates.

Demographics for a Batch of Prospects at Once

If you attempt to locate information on a large number of prospects at once for an annual fund appeal or database cleanup, you want to look into the services of the following companies for

> For one development office project back in the day, my roommate was assigned to go through old yearbooks from the 1950s through 1970s and attempt to locate and identify how many African American athletes there were in each sport. The information was "there" in school records, but not in our database, and the particular project called for that information. So we spent our evenings looking at pictures in yearbooks and keeping a tally. It made for a fun way to spend summer evenings, and the development office got some great data added to the database.
>
> **stories from the real world**

batch information appends. A number of years ago, our institution did a wealth screening of a significant portion of the database through GG+A and, as part of that screening, we got a file with the names and ages of children of our alumni.

Many of the companies will provide you with biographical information appends.

◆ Blackbaud

◆ Accurint

◆ Wealth Engine

◆ GG+A (Grenzebach Glier and Associates)

To Recap

◆ Though fundamental, demographics can change frequently.

◆ There are myriad free and fee-based one-off searches.

◆ Most major subscription services have data append capability.

Chapter Fourteen

General Philanthropy

IN THIS CHAPTER

···→ Fee-based services for philanthropy

···→ Free sources for philanthropy

Often, determining people's philanthropic values (that is, *what* they value, not the monetary value) really helps your organization determine the best way to approach prospects about giving. For this reason, it is really helpful to know where else they give and the level at which they give to places that are similar to and different from you. You won't find everything, of course, but you can often learn a lot about inclinations through the use of both free and fee-based services.

Sources to which You Subscribe

If you start with a fee-based service (like NOZA, or Prospect Research Online, or Wealth Engine), they will often compile the giving for you in a report. This report includes the recipient organization, the year, the gift level (often not an actual gift amount, but a range, like $500–

These fee-based aggregators can be of great value to your shop, especially if you don't have a lot of time to comb through information. What can take mere minutes through a paid service (because the online "bot" has done the legwork for you) can take hours if you're trying to find annual reports on your own. If funds are tight, *free* might be the way to go. But if you can swing it financially, these resources are invaluable.

The annual report can provide your organization with important information about both donors and recipients. You will begin to see connections between different people and organizations based on where the money is going. In a corporate annual report or tax document, you will often find a list of who received gifts from a prospect in a given year and what types of projects they supported. (A nonprofit's annual report will state who it received money *from*, and a corporation's annual report will state who it gave money *to*. These are both valuable pieces of information to a researcher.)

$999), and maybe a link to the information source. Generally, this information comes from online annual reports from organizations or press releases from those organizations. Go through each of these gifts on the report to determine whether they are, in fact, your prospects. There are many people named John and Mary Smith!

Other options for researching philanthropy for your prospects with subscription services work much like a wealth screening. Some vendors also conduct a philanthropy screening for individuals in your database. When you perform this screening, you're not getting values on what they *could* give (capacity). Instead, you find data about where they *do* give. Through listserves or your contact resources (that you compiled in the section on Foundations), check with individuals at organizations similar to yours for which vendors that might match up best with your organization's goals and financial resources. This type of screening can be very useful in determining what sorts of projects are of interest to your prospects.

Free Philanthropy Resources

If you decide to start with a free service, a web search engine is a great way to do it. You can choose whichever service you like best and then create a search string that will help you filter out philanthropy.

A few years ago, someone from a listserve sent me the search string that she uses to find donations. You put the name in quotes and then add a Boolean phrase to include words like "Donor," "Gift," "Donation," "Annual Report," "Steward," "Generous," or other key words to narrow the results.

Some organizations publish their annual reports online, and you can search for your prospect's name this way. Some organizations do not put these reports on the Internet and publish only on paper. Some organizations have stopped publishing donor lists altogether, mostly for privacy reasons or for cost savings in an effort to better steward donor money. In some cases, organizations have stopped publishing donor lists because the donors don't want them anymore. The recognition or information available in an annual report or donor list is no longer important to those donors. But until annual reports and donor lists go away completely, they are great resources for compiling a more complete picture of your donor's interests and philanthropic capabilities.

We find it very helpful to use this special trick when searching or Googling for a prospect's philanthropic donations. When you put the prospect's name in quotations (as mentioned above) in the search engine, use the following formats, as donors are very commonly listed this way in annual reports and donor lists:

◆ "Mr. and Mrs. John X. Doe"

◆ "Mr. & Mrs. John X. Doe"

◆ "Mr. and/& Mrs. John Doe"

◆ "Dr. and/& Mrs. John and Jane Doe"

◆ "John X. and/& Jane X. Doe"

◆ "Butch and/& Janie Doe"—for more informal organizations, neighborhood groups, etc.

Surely you get a sense of the patterns by now. And, yes, it seems like many permutations. But this extra effort will yield the most complete information for your prospects.

Compiling Philanthropy Data

Once you have the data, you have to figure out how to return it to the fundraiser in a useful form (remember the profile templates you created in the section on Foundations? They will come in handy here).

When I compile philanthropic history in a donor profile or research results, I like to format it as a set of bullet points, with the year as the left-most category.

2010:

◆ $5,000+ level

   ◆ St. Louis Zoo

   ◆ Washington University

◆ $1,000–$4,999 level

   ◆ St. Louis Children's Hospital

   ◆ St. Louis Art Museum

◆ $0–99 level

   ◆ Seattle Art Festival

It's always good to ask analytical questions when you're compiling data. So I might say something like this when I look at that data: "Hmm . . . make a note to check on the gifts to the Seattle Art Festival. The donor's other giving is all around St. Louis. And why did that giving change so significantly from 2009 to 2010? Where does giving to your organization fit within these lists? It's also possible that it's for another person with the same name . . ."

2009:

- ◆ $5,000+ level
  - ◆ Seattle Art Festival
- ◆ $1,000–$4,999 level
  - ◆ St. Louis Children's Hospital
  - ◆ Washington University
- ◆ $250–$499 level
  - ◆ St. Louis Zoo
  - ◆ St. Louis Art Museum

Organizing gifts in this way allows you to see what is most closely aligned with the donor's values right now as opposed to what the donor has supported in the past. You might also want to organize it by recipient type (e.g., all medical facilities together, all education institutions together, all art organizations together) or by gift level. The important thing to remember when listing philanthropy is to have it in some sort of order that makes sense to your organization or the fundraiser requesting the information.

When using philanthropy as a research tool for foundational (annual fund) prospects, you will most likely be trying to determine the best ask level. If you notice that the prospect has many gifts that are over $5,000, and your annual fund has been asking them for gifts of $250, you can probably increase your ask amount. If, on the other hand, the prospect has continually declined gifts at the $1,000 level to your organization, and you notice that they have many annual gifts to other organizations at the level around $50–$100, then you might want to adjust your ask downward a bit to get a more favorable response. Although many people are not offended if you think they could give you a lot more than they actually could, some people are more sensitive to high ask amounts, so if you're asking for a lot and not getting a positive response, you might want to ask for less to re-engage the prospect with your organization. You might also suggest getting them involved in volunteer activities to re-engage them.

> Remember that one of the key fundraising tenets is asking for the right amount for the right purpose at the right time. Researching the prospect's general philanthropy elsewhere will really help you clarify what those characteristics are.
>
> For example, your prospect gives mostly to education-oriented charities, so you might want to talk to the prospect about the new children's classroom you want to build; or your prospect just made a $50,000 pledge to the church capital campaign, so you might want to wait a year or two to make your ask.
>
> **principle**

> Never underestimate the connections to be found when companies are making gifts in your community—you might be looking up annual reports to see where Company TEX is listed as a donor, and lo-and-behold, you also find mentions of JAG Corporation and the Raindrop Foundation, which are also on your prospect list. Remember to add those pieces of philanthropic data to your database in the appropriate places as well. You just researched a couple of additional companies without even trying!
>
> **practical tip**

So, since annual reports are so important to our research on philanthropy, here's a few ideas about how to get them:

> Researching prospects and providing complete profiles helps your institution be a good steward of the gifts your donors have entrusted to you.
>
> practical tip

◆ Exchanges with other organizations with whom you share many donors or donor groups (this might be the case if you are in a large metropolitan area and have several museums, art galleries or theaters who all attract the same types of people).

◆ Getting on the mailing list for the organization. This can be a bit of a sticky point, because you do not want to pretend to be interested in an organization in order to mine its donors. That would be a violation of the ethics statements of our profession.

◆ Someone in your organization may be involved with the other organization as a volunteer or donor and routinely receive information. In this case, is it OK, and ethical, to ask that individual to share a copy to look up your prospect's information.

An important point in this discussion is that you are gathering information on the charitable giving of your prospects and donors because you want to ensure that you are approaching them about giving opportunities *that interest them*, and/or they are capable of a major gift, and/or they are philanthropically inclined. You are not trying to trick them or get them to give to something they would not want to give to. By researching these prospects and providing complete profiles, you help your institution properly steward the gifts with which they have been entrusted.

To Recap

◆ Knowing where donors give helps identify their values.

◆ Use free and fee sources to locate philanthropy.

◆ Compile philanthropy data in a logical fashion to make it tell a story.

Chapter Fifteen

Political Giving

Not a political organization? It's still important information to include. Political giving will help you paint the picture of the prospect as a whole person. You will see how the prospect is involved with the local community, and maybe you can even determine what sorts of issues that individual finds important.

The Importance of Political Giving

Political giving also offers you insights into a donor's political mindset, which could be vital information if a gift officer who will visit the prospect is at the opposite end of the spectrum. Having this knowledge allows you to be sensitive to content of the discussions with your prospects. You don't have to specifically *use* this information for it to be useful. Sometimes just knowing it in the back of your mind can help you appropriately frame your discussions with prospects.

Locating Political Gifts

Political giving can turn up in multiple types of searches. Newsmeat (newsmeat.com) allows you to search by name and location, or a more general location search allows you to browse the gifts from that area.

Fundrace from the Huffington Post (fundrace.huffingtonpost.com) will also show you a summary of a prospect's political giving, including the amount, year, and candidate(s) supported.

Cara's favorite site for federal political donations is CQ Moneyline, from the Congressional Quarterly. I just like the layout: tray.com/pml/home.do

Example

Another valuable source is OpenSecrets (opensecrets.org), which shows all of the supporters for a specific candidate during a particular election cycle.

A simple web search for the prospect's name and "political giving" or "political campaign" may also yield results.

Political giving at the state and local level can also be found at your state's campaign finance office, though we mention these as a secondary resource because they are, honestly, just not as user friendly. I have found it very hard to actually find the websites themselves. And I've also found that the sites can be quite slow.

A few states make it easy to search donations by name, or address, or employer, or a whole bunch of other data points. But other states allow searching only by candidate (if the information is available online at all). So, unless you know who your prospect donated to, it would take far too much time to sort through innumerable candidates looking for one person's contributions.

Here are the links to a few larger state campaign finance sites. If your state is not listed here, look at these first, so you know what to look for in any other state:

◆ Illinois: elections.il.gov/CampaignDisclosure/ ContributionsSearchByAllContributions.aspx

◆ California (this one is strangely hard to find): dbsearch.ss.ca.gov/ContributorSearch. aspx

◆ Texas: ethics.state.tx.us/php/cesearchAdvanced.html

◆ Florida (scroll down to get to the contributor section): election.dos.state.fl.us/ campaign-finance/contrib.asp

To Recap

◆ Political giving isn't important just for political organizations

◆ Political campaign gifts can identify donor values

Chapter Sixteen

Foundational Prospects

IN THIS CHAPTER

···→ Components of a profile for Foundational Prospects

···→ Suggested layout for initial profile

In the previous five chapters, we've been exploring the components that make up the information you'll almost always need when you're creating a research profile. These prospects are often considered annual fund prospects, but the principles learned here will apply regardless of what level of prospect you are researching.

Each of the five preceding chapters detailed one section of this profile. First we learned about what makes up a connection to our organization. In the profile that follows, you will see that there are several ideas for university constituencies. Please feel free to adapt these ideas to fit the specifics of your organization. A few of the bullet points include follow-up questions to help guide your thinking about what makes a complete set of information. The next section is pretty self-explanatory and gives you ideas for all of the permutations that contact information can take. You never know which contact information will be the best when you're just starting out, so try to keep whatever you find in this section. Part Three will give you a sample layout for philanthropic gifts to other organizations. As you get more comfortable with higher-level prospects, you'll find that this section gets a lot more detailed, so it's a great idea to set up a plan from the outset to keep the information logical and neat. Finally, Part Four is where you'll summarize your findings regarding political giving. Again, this will get more important as you move forward with higher-level prospects, but it's a good idea to start it now.

Sample Template for Foundational Prospect

Section 1: Connections to Our University

- ❏ Alumnus (When was graduation? More than one degree? What field?)
- ❏ Parent (To whom?)
- ❏ Board member
- ❏ Student
- ❏ Volunteer (With what programs?)
- ❏ Employee (In what department/s?)
- ❏ Former employee (When was retirement or resignation?)
- ❏ Specific names of individual connections within our institution
- ❏ Other connections

Section 2: Contact Information

- ❏ Street address, city, and state of primary home address
- ❏ Street address, city, and state of any additional residences (If these are seasonal, do you have dates when the individual tends to be at these addresses?)
- ❏ Street address, city, and state of primary business address
- ❏ Street address, city, and state of any additional business addresses (Owner of multiple businesses? Offices in more than one location?)
- ❏ Primary home phone number
- ❏ Primary personal cell phone number
- ❏ Primary business phone number
- ❏ Primary business cell number
- ❏ Primary personal email address
- ❏ Primary business address
- ❏ Notation about which contact preferred

Section 3: General Philanthropy

- ❏ Gifts above $5,000: Organization (Location), Year
- ❏ Gifts between $1,000 and $4,999: Organization (Location), Year
- ❏ Gifts between $500 and $999: Organization (Location), Year

❑ Gifts between $100 and $499: Organization (Location), Year

❑ Gifts up to $99: Organization (Location), Year

❑ Unspecified Amount Gifts: Organization (Location), Year

Section 4: Political Giving

❑ Candidate, Year, Amount, Type

❑ Party Registration

Hopefully the information above will start your thinking and give you a framework for implementing your own profiles for foundational prospects. You'll find yourself coming back to these sections time and again as you create research profiles for prospects at all levels.

To Recap

◆ Templates give you a framework to organize information so fundraisers can find it.

◆ Always include connections, contact information, philanthropy, and political giving in a profile.

◆ Start implementing a template now.

Part Three

Middle of the Road—Major Gifts Start Here

In chapters 17 through 22, we explore the "Middle of the Road." The Middle of the Road is an interesting place. It can be where millionaires are hiding. Or it can be the place where you find your future big donors, who are still climbing the career ladder or having kids, etc. There will be plenty of prospects here who won't give to your organization, or won't give much, but it's the place to start building your major gift prospect pool.

What is a "major" gift? Different organizations define major gifts very differently. I've worked in places where a major gift was $100,000 or greater. Others, where it was $25,000 or greater. And some, where $5,000 made a big ("major") difference. And you may not be the person who decides what a major gift is for your organization.

What is important is that, as a researcher or the person who is doing some side research into your prospects, you should focus your efforts on whoever you think qualifies as a major gift donor. You can't research everyone, and if you somehow managed to, you'd be wasting your time. The point of prospect research is to focus fundraising efforts on the prospects who will give you the best return on investment on time spent researching.

4
The
Big
Leagues
•Stocks
•Salary •Company
•Franchises
•Charitable Foundation
•Luxury Items

3 - Middle of the Road

•Real Estate   •Affiliations

•Family   •Interests   •Capacity

2 - Foundational Prospects
•Connections   •Contacts
•Demographics & Public Records
•General Philanthropy & Political Giving

1 - Foundations
•Database   •Templates   •Glossary   •Resources
•Data Mining & Predictive Modeling   •Ethics and Laws
•Pyramids & Ranking   •Bonus Features

Chapter Seventeen

Real Estate

IN THIS CHAPTER

- ···→ Why use real estate
- ···→ Where to find real estate data
- ···→ How to value real estate

The first place to start is with real estate. It's *the* foundational piece of information to get when you are looking at a prospect for major gift potential.

Why is it the foundational piece of information to get? For the most part, because it is the easiest to find. Most real estate information is available online, free of charge. And most people who are capable of giving a major gift own some.

Also, because it is a relatively simple thing to estimate net worth based on total real estate. There are some quick and easy formulas you can memorize to help you do this. But we'll get to that in a bit.

Does Your Prospect Own More than Just a Home?

If your prospect owns a primary residence, PLUS another property, that is very often a sign that your prospect falls into the major gift category. People who can maintain and pay taxes on second properties usually have enough assets to at least consider a major gift.

There are exceptions to every rule—your prospect might have been sold swampland infested with alligators and rats and now has no way to unload it. But situations in which a second property is a drag on a prospect's finances are the exception, not the rule. Here are some points to keep in mind:

◆ If the property is a vacation home, it's a pretty solid bet that the owner is capable of making a major gift (even if not necessarily willing).

◆ If the property is a rental—well, then there's rental income that you can consider in estimating the prospect's wealth/net worth.

◆ Commercial property is another pretty solid indicator of wealth.

◆ Large tracts of land/acreage can be sold for development (usually at a very pretty penny) or rented for farming use (again, another source of income).

If you know that your prospect owns property in addition to a primary residence, then it's a smart bet to investigate the value of property owned, even if you can get the value of the residence only. You know that there are other assets to consider, and that's a good thing.

Finding Real Estate Data

Let's start with the quick and easy, though not always completely accurate, way. A variety of sites allow you to look up real estate information, and most of them are the sites that anyone can use when they are shopping for real estate! You may have already used some of them yourself—and we prospect researchers don't want or need to reinvent the wheel.

Most of these sites are simply listing houses for sale in any given area, and if you have a site covering your area that you like a lot, use it! But these are not realtor specific sites. They list all the sales in the area, no matter who is selling (even sometimes For Sale By Owner). Some common websites are

◆ zillow.com (provides an estimated value based on proprietary formula)

◆ realestate.msn.com

◆ blockshopper.com (then by city or borough, does not have all areas of the United States, just major cities and metropolitan areas)

◆ redfin.com (also does not have all areas)

What can greatly improve your estimate is looking at what houses next door or nearby sell for—or, as realtors say, *comparables*. For example, find another Tudor-style house,

Most of you probably already know all this stuff, but if you are a complete newbie to real estate and know nothing about buying and selling and valuing it— that's an entirely different book. You can probably surf a few websites and get a good enough understanding of what it's all about. So we're not going to cover that here.

observation

with a similar square footage and similar features (e.g., pools, two-car garages, decks, etc.), that is for sale now or has recently sold.

If you are using this method, visit two or three of these sites to find comparable properties. And base the estimated value of your prospect's real estate holdings on a compilation of all of those comparables. You should be able to put together a pretty darn solid estimate for any and all property or properties that you know the prospect owns.

This method, unfortunately, can get tricky in rural areas. First, many of these sites don't have information for the most rural areas. And some rural areas don't even put this sort of information online at all, in any format. Or maybe your prospect has a ski chalet about ten miles outside of Vail, which might be off the map and outside the main residential areas that these sites cover. That can happen, but the next method of finding real estate data can help you find what you are looking for. It's the more detailed method, which will take a bit more time (though not always).

Going Straight to the Source for Real Estate Values

If you didn't already know, property values in the United States are calculated at the county level. And each county may or may not maintain a website at which you can look up property values for, at the least, all residential properties. Some sites also list commercial and vacant properties, but not all.

Property values are public information, covered by most state "sunshine" laws. So it's likely you'll be able to find your prospect's property using this search method.

> Not every county has a property assessor website. Some, especially the most rural counties, don't yet have searchable, online databases for showing property assessments. If there is a website at all, it may just list contact information for the assessor's office, and if you like, you can call for the information and actually talk to a real person. It is public information, and everyone has the right to call for it.
>
>

Assessment Site (pulawski.net)

This is Cara's starting point, *always*. A fantastic and seasoned prospect research professional maintains this site, with the help of any and all other prospect research professionals willing to take the time to send in updates. (The email is at the bottom of the home page—all are welcome!) It's kind of the Wikipedia of property assessment. It is a state by state, and then county by county (or township by township, borough by borough, or island by island—yes, Hawaii), listing of property assessors for every state in the Union.

Now, county property databases vary greatly, and that's why the Pulawski site is so great. It often provides some extra context for the state or county (city or borough, etc.), as needed, or alternate sites to search if a given county does not have a database. There are some property assessment sites out there that work for counties to provide the data (the county pays these Internet companies to make their data publicly available).

If you have any of the paid subscription services, such as Wealth Engine, iWave Prospect Research Online, LexisNexis for Development Professionals, Research Point, etc., you can often find the PIN for a property within the real estate search results. So if you don't have it when you first start your prospect research, go back to these assessor sites later after you've checked some other places and found these pieces of data.

And also (sorry if this is getting complicated, but that's how it is dealing with hundreds of counties across all 50 states), *what* you can search for in each database will vary greatly. In many databases, you can search by a variety of criteria, like name, address, property ID number (PIN), zip code, etc. Some allow you to search by address only. In others, you must search by the PIN only.

Assessment Multipliers

So, once you get to the assessor information, you're going to see data on "multipliers."

Many counties and states use a "multiplier" to calculate assessment value. This means that the assessed value is a fraction of what the market value of a property is. The multiplier is used mainly to keep taxes down, especially in areas where property values are at a premium, like beaches, big cities, and highly desirable areas.

The methods of calculating them are quite complex, but all you need to know is this formula:

(assessed value) x (that area's multiplier) = approximate market value of the property

OR

$121,598 x 3.28 = $398,841

Multipliers work the same in all states EXCEPT for California, which has a very unique system for calculating home value. You can research and try to understand it if you like but, frankly, I recommend not using the assessed value for homes in California. Just try to find the market value using a combination of the first method we describe in this chapter and assessor's listings from the second method, because some of the sites provide photo of the properties, and that's always helpful.

Also, most counties in California block the owner's name on property records, because of a privacy and safety law enacted in 2002 (CA AB2238). So you have to search by address or PIN. I find this unfortunate for us prospect researchers, since there's a *lot* of wealth in California! *C'est la vie*!

It's always a bonus when you can search an assessor's site by name, because then you can find all the properties a prospect owns in that county if it's more than just a home. You might find listings for:

◆ Additional properties—land that is not the primary (or even secondary) residence

◆ Farmland owned that they could sell to developers and/or receive subsidies on

◆ Rental and other income properties

Now that we've gotten through how to figure out the value of real estate, let's take a few minutes to look at how that factors in to our net worth equation.

Formulas for Using Real Estate to Calculate Total Net Worth or Total Wealth

The IRS creates data, usually after each census, that provides a statistical outlook on wealth and income in the United States. And from this, they have gleaned formulas to estimate wealth. The foremost of interest to us is the following:

Total real estate holdings generally represent twenty percent of a wealthy person's total wealth portfolio.

This applies to people in higher income brackets and *not* the average working person whose only asset of significance is a home. But you probably aren't researching the "average working person." You are hopefully (and really should only be) looking at wealthy prospects for whom you already have information indicating they are "wealthy" in whatever terms you define wealth in your organization.

If you want another qualifier to help define wealthy, use this formula only for prospects whose primary residences are valued at $500,000 or greater. (If your prospect is in a large and expensive city like New York or San Francisco, or a tony resort town like Vail, Colorado, you should probably raise this value to $750,000 or $1 million or greater.)

To Recap

◆ Real estate is a foundational piece of wealth data.

◆ Choose resources that make sense for your organization.

◆ Use common formulas to translate real estate holdings into net worth.

Chapter Eighteen

Affiliations, Boards, and Committees

IN THIS CHAPTER

···→ Corporate vs. charitable affiliations

···→ Where to find this information

Another indicator of potential wealth is membership on boards or committees. There are basically two kinds—professional (or corporate) and charitable (or volunteer). And there are varying types for both.

A prospect can serve on a board for any company that cares to set one up. And if a prospect serves on the board of a large and publicly traded corporation, then you can discover what kind of compensation the prospect receives and how much. But we will cover that in the stock chapter of the next section, the Big Leagues. Here, we'll deal with the latter kind, the charitable, or volunteer, boards.

Board Membership Philanthropy Requirements

There are many levels of involvement and volunteerism—but fairly often, board service has a financial gift requirement. Most larger charitable organizations require that all board members make a gift of some kind annually. The larger the organization, the larger the amount required. For example, for the board of a mid- to large-sized university, in which case the prospect might be called a trustee, requirements might range from $1,000 to $10,000 annually, up to $100,000 for very large or very prestigious universities.

The same goes for large and prestigious arts organizations, hospitals, or other charities. Not all of them require such gifts, so there is no guarantee that your prospect is making a gift. The best way to check if your prospect is contributing financially is in an annual report, if one is

In some institutions, board members are required to fundraise a certain amount of money each year, and this can be in lieu of a personal gift. This approach is slightly less common, and the amount they are required to bring in varies widely. But it would be an indicator that they run in more wealthy circles.

food for thought

available. Many organizations publish their annual reports online, and you can check the organization's website.

If you can determine the amount or range of the required contribution, use it as you would any other gift amount to calculate a prospect's net worth.

Locating Board Member Giving

In the previous section of chapters, "Foundational Prospects," we went into detail about how and where to find listings of a prospect's charitable giving. Here we will just list again the most common sources/websites for finding this information:

◆ nozasearch.com

◆ iWave.com

◆ targetanalytics.com

◆ lndp.com

◆ Searching your favorite search engine for names with "gift" or "donor" (see previous chapter discussion, "General Philanthropy," for how to search this information)

Annual reports sometimes publish the amount donors contribute annually or, most often, the total giving range in which a donor qualifies for that year. But it is usually difficult to find out exactly how much the financial contribution is. It's not the kind of thing most organizations publish.

While researching a company recently that is on target for a $50,000 ask, I found a number of gifts they made to other higher-education institutions as well as a number of other gifts at every level from up to $1,000 to over $500,000. I could tell that, in general, most higher-education institutions received grants in the $10,000 to $50,000 range, unless they had a specific focus on animal rights in one of the science departments, and that the larger gifts tended to go to national organizations that were helping individuals and animals in need. When I returned the research results to the fundraiser, I did not include every single gift the company made. I included gifts to education institutions that were greater than $1,000 and large gifts to other organizations in the area near us.

stories from the real world

If you know someone within the organization, it is not unethical to ask for the information or for that person to share it, assuming the individual is willing and has authority to do so. That person may expect you to share *your* donor information in return, though, and you should assure the individual that any information provided to you will remain confidential within your development team. In general, though, the gift range can be just as beneficial to you as the specific amount.

Summaries of philanthropy are also very helpful for Middle of the Road prospects, because they will help you determine if your organization is similar to what they usually fund and at what level they tend to fund initiatives such as yours.

To Recap

◆ Charitable affiliations often indicate wealth.

◆ Internet resources can uncover these connections.

Chapter Nineteen

Family and Significant Relationships

IN THIS CHAPTER

    ···→ Why family and relationships are important

    ···→ Where to find relationship data

    ···→ Legacy families

    ···→ Ways to track relationships

There are multiple reasons to research family and significant relationships for your prospects and donors. This chapter will examine why these are important, how to find out about them, and how to connect the information within your organization.

Reasons to Investigate Family Relationships

It is sometimes worthwhile to investigate a prospect's family and/or significant relationships. If a prospect had wealthy parents, the prospect may have received or be in line for a significant inheritance. Other members of the family (parents, siblings) may be wealthy and have foundations or charitable trusts willing to make donations on behalf of your prospect.

Or your prospect may be able to convince several family members to make a combination gift, and their combined efforts could amount to what qualifies as a major gift or could increase the size of their major gift.

Q: Is using obituaries for research necessary, or is it morbid?

A: Frankly, we think it's necessary. Obituaries contain in just a few lines of text a great deal of information about family and/or connections.

   Many obituaries also cite an organization that the deceased would like memorial gifts send to—and that organization could be yours! So it's good to learn in advance to expect those memorial gifts.

Q: How much information do you put in your database?

A: At one organization, we copied the entire obituary, including the link to the source, as an attachment document in our database. At another organization, we simply updated the record as *deceased* and entered a date. Another option is to copy the relevant pieces of family information, career information, and other items that connect the person to your organization, and enter those as contact reports in your system.

On the flip side, it is important to know if other family members represent a drain on a prospect's financial resources. Does your prospect have a teenage child about to enter college? Does your prospect help support an aging parent or an ailing or disabled sibling? These are the two most common ways we've found that family can present an encumbrance on finances, but there are certainly other ways in which family members can draw upon your prospect's wealth.

Maybe your prospect has a special connection to someone in your organization and is inclined to make a gift for that person's project or area of interest—for example, a former professor who made a huge difference in the prospect's learning experience or career goals. Or a doctor who took special care of the prospect during a time of need.

Another reason you might want to investigate these relationships is simply the idea of networking. The more people you identify, the more likely you are to find the best connections. We address networks more in coming chapters because they become even more important when you're researching people in the Big Leagues.

Locating Family and Relationship Data

Finding this information can be tricky, though the more common pieces are often publicly available.

The best place to start looking for information on family connections and significant relationships is in your own files and database. There are a few other common sites that establish these connections, listed below:

Checklist for heirs:

❏ Your database and/or central files

❏ Social Security death index

❏ Accurint

❏ Newspaper obituaries

❏ Media articles and profiles

Children

If a prospect has very young children, they won't be listed in phone books, on property records, etc. Usually, young adults aren't listed in public records until they acquire a driver's license or turn eighteen and register to vote or reach some other milestone. So information on young children is usually gathered via anecdotal evidence (conversations, correspondence, etc.) from fundraising officers, various staff members, and others.

Sometimes young children are listed in obituaries, but not always. Adult children are usually listed individually, but more often than not, young children/grandchildren are noted only as a total number, like "six grandchildren and two great-grandchildren."

Most professional researchers shy away from social networking sites as a means to gather information on a prospect. It can be (or feel like) a serious violation of privacy. As a general rule, use only what a person makes available to the general public on such sites.

DO *not* friend a prospect or the prospect's family members unless you know them personally and they know who you are and what you do (fundraising research). A caveat might be if you have a professional page on these sites and, therefore, people have full knowledge of what they are sharing with you when you connect with them.

Though more often than not, if you know someone, even a prospect, well enough to link to via social networking, it's unlikely you would be soliciting that person for a gift anyway.

This is a constantly evolving topic right now, so be sure to keep up with the online discussion forums with APRA, AASP, CASE, and AFP to see how it unfolds.

important

If a prospect's children are in their teens, they are sometimes found on the Internet via media reports on school accomplishments or activities (e.g., sports, honor roll, arts events). And/or those teenagers are putting themselves out on the Internet, via Facebook, MySpace, or other websites. They might even have their own websites.

Legacy Families

When soliciting a prospect, it can be very important for you to know if the individual belongs to what is called a "legacy family." In this situation, succeeding generations of a family have

I, Cara Rosson, swear this is true. Cross my heart!

One of the universities I worked for received a check in the mail one day from an attorney's office in Florida. The check was for over $7 million! The letter with the check indicated that the gift was from a person's estate, but it held no other details. The person whose estate the check came from was unknown to anyone in our department—to anyone in the administration, for that matter—and certainly wasn't in our database.

A call to the attorney's office by our vice president's secretary did not yield much information, either, as the decedent was very elderly and he not know this person well. He could say, though, that we had received the bulk of the estate because the son had spoken very well of his time at our university, and apparently the love of our university stuck with him, even though there was no other gift of record.

Long story short, it took me several hours of searching to discover that the decedent's son attended our university for about a year and a half before being drafted and sent to Vietnam, where he was sadly killed in battle. The decedent's fortune was made many years ago (read: pre-Internet publishing) in an unusual industry, and I consider myself quite lucky to have found an article about it! Great thanks to Google and my own Internet research know-how.

Now, I'm not saying that this situation will happen to you. It's pretty darn unlikely. I simply repeat it here as a cautionary tale of how it can be quite valuable to track family information!

stories from
the real world

donated to your organization. This fact greatly increases the likelihood of giving and, if possible, can greatly increase the amount of a major gift—especially if the family combines resources to make one large gift.

Knowing who the members of a prospect's family are is also important if you are the beneficiary of a will or other planned gift. I've lost count of the times we've had to look up decades-old obituary records to determine the names of descendants to see whether we will be receiving a planned gift. In some cases, the copy of the will we received specified that we would get a remainder of the trust after the children and spouses pass away, so we needed to determine whether they were alive and where they were located so we could continue to steward the family.

In some cases, you need to find family members to get their feedback on whether you need to update or change a written gift statement. Perhaps in the 1970s, your institution worked with a donor to set up an endowment. Now, in 2012, the original project no longer fits with the direction of your institution, so you need to refine the payout guidelines so you can continue to utilize the earnings from that account. However, if the donors are since deceased, you will need to locate family members to get their approval of the proposed changes.

> Perhaps you are asked to determine whether John A. Franklin and John Franklin in your database are the same individual. Seems easy enough to pull some records, do a little quick searching, and determine whether these records represent one or two individuals. However, if you take just a few minutes more, you might discover there is also a record for Jon A. Franklin in your database (who, incidentally, *is* the same as the "John" you were asked about), and that there are records in your database for a spouse (married to the "Jon" record) and three children, even though none of these connections are written concretely in your system.
>
> Maybe it took you an hour longer to figure this out, but you have accomplished some really important work for future endeavors. In addition to your duplicate research, you cleaned up a couple of records, deleted a duplicate record, found a spouse, and connected three children and spouses. Pretty good return on that hour, don't you think?
>
> **Example**

Relationship Mapping

Some of the research products out there are really getting involved now with relationship mapping, so it's becoming easier to research these types of relationships. You can even get graphical representations of the connections between people and groups. As you research higher-capacity donors, you will find that relationships are a hugely important aspect of the work, and it's a good idea to spend some time now figuring out how to keep track of these relationships.

Here is a true story where knowing who the prospect's family members were would have saved a lot of people from a somewhat embarrassing situation.

The phonathon students (who call for annual fund gifts from everyone not assigned to a major gift officer) were trained to opt for the "polite, formal" name when asking to speak with the prospects. So the student called, a woman answered the phone, and the student asked, "Is Ms. Brown there?" The woman answered that she is Ms. Brown. So the student asked her for a gift of $150, which was the general ask for new grads. The woman said "Well, since I just named the science complex, I don't believe I'll be doing that right now." (ACK!)

The next day, someone in the admissions office asked the student's boss's boss, "Why did you call my mother, who is on the board, and ask her for $150?" This, of course, came back to the phonathon director's desk. Indeed, we were trying to contact the *sister* of the employee, and the *daughter* of the woman who answered the phone.

Luckily, she was amused once she discovered what was going on. But it could have gone *very* wrong. We also reminded the phonathon students to specify *which* Ms. Brown they are asking for. It is still polite and formal if you say, "Ms. Amy Brown," and then you ensure that you get the person you want to talk to. Or, at the very least, if they know about the family tree, they will know to verify which Ms. Brown they are talking to before they make the ask.

stories from
the real world

Some tips you might use to track these relationships:

◆ Actually link the records together in your database with the appropriate relationship categories.

◆ Include lists of networks, contacts, and family in your contact reports as a separate type.

◆ Use some sort of cloud computing software to create graphic representations of connections.

◆ If you're a small organization and don't have a huge database, create your own network diagrams on a wall or on a series of posters.

Another tip for relationship research is to do a little bit more research than required for a specific request. ("What?" you ask. "I don't have time to do extra research. I'm barely keeping my head above water here!" To which we reply, "Ah, but you should take the extra few minutes in this case.")

To Recap

◆ Family and relationships can establish strong connections to your organization.

◆ Researching and tracking relationships can help refine gift asks.

Chapter Twenty

Personal and Shared Interests

IN THIS CHAPTER

···→ Why personal and shared interests are important

···→ Where to find interest information

Statistically, over and over, studies show that one of the top reasons for giving is because people care—about your organization, the cause you are working for, your mission and purpose, etc. Reasons like tax breaks and tradition usually come in second to passions and interests. So, looking at your prospects for similar concerns and interests is a great way to prioritize prospects and hone in on what program or aspect of your organization will appeal to them.

Aligning your prospects' specific interests carefully with your program or funding needs increases the likelihood they will invest in what you ask them to by a large percentage.

A regular donor started her career as a fourth grade teacher but now runs her own educational printing company. Might she be interested in giving to your educational programming?

A regular donor is a triathlete. Could that person be interested in giving toward a new training center, gymnasium, or athletic equipment for your students, or to your program that funds athletic experience camps for the disabled or the elderly?

Example

Locating Donor Interest Data

It is not unusual that major gift donors will give to organizations that reflect their interests and passions. So review the section above, affiliations, boards, and committees, for some suggestions.

But, often, interests do not reflect giving (e.g., a passion for French cooking). And unfortunately, there are as many places to search as there are individual interests. But we can give you a few hints on where to start looking:

> It is a really good idea to remind your development officers to make note of prospect interests when they go on visits. When out talking to prospects, there are probably many mentions indicating what the prospect is interested in, and you can detect passions within the objects in and style of homes and offices. Work on your relationship with gift officers so they remember to feed information back to you about interests. If you have general ideas, you'll get clues about where to look for other ideas.

- ◆ Internal records—Do you have a file of correspondence with this person in which you can look for these details? Do you or anyone else in your organization have notes about the prospect? Any kind of internal records—even photographs—can provide clues.

- ◆ Personal knowledge—Does anyone in your organization know the prospect personally? They might be able to provide a few clues or suggestions.

- ◆ Media articles—You might find articles detailing the prospect's recent travel adventures or love of quilting. Search your local newspaper, business journal, or magazine websites for the person's name.

- ◆ Online search—Google (or use your preferred Internet search engine, of course). There might be a website about historical research into your town's origins, or your prospect might be listed as a member of the local specialty car club. Note: Please remember our warning in the last chapter—we advise against linking to prospects on social networks unless you know them personally. What they make available to the general public, though, is fair to use.

Personal and shared interests are actually a great tandem research segment to relationship mapping. And by connecting the two, you are also doing a bit of data modeling on the side. (Woohoo! Multitasking! Look at you go!)

So, if you know of several connections between your prospect and other prospects or donors in your database, you can start looking at those overlapping connections to identify some interests. If all of a prospect's friends have given to museum openings, perhaps the prospect would be interested in that too. This is also a good reason to do philanthropy research before interests, since where money goes tends to imply (or shout) what interests the prospect.

To Recap

◆ Align prospect interests with organizational priorities.

◆ Find and track interest information to help build stronger prospect networks.

◆ More connections are correlated with likelihood of larger major gifts.

Chapter Twenty-One

Determining General Capacity Range

IN THIS CHAPTER

···→ What is general capacity?

···→ How to calculate a general capacity range

When we speak of *capacity*, we generally refer to the level at which a donor could give a *stretch gift* over a period of five years (or a combined amount) to favorite charities. There are a few standard formulas for calculating prospect wealth and capacity range.

Though, frankly, neither one of us depends much on these formulas, if at all. They are useful as a vague guideline, but as you research any given prospect, hopefully you will get a much better sense of giving capacity than by using these rough formulas.

Useful Formulas for Net Worth and Capacity Ratings

A common formula, given by Thomas Stanley and William Danko in their book, *The Millionaire Next Door*, is:

Age x total income / 10 = net worth

Most researchers find that this formula provides a very conservative estimate. You should look at other factors to determine if your prospect is philanthropic and where they are on the scale from lavish to frugal. Of course, this also depends on you knowing the prospect's income, which is possible only

> Stretch Gift—A donor normally needs to think about a stretch gift before just pulling out a checkbook and writing you a check and might even want to first discuss it with a financial advisor.
>
>

if the prospect is high up in a company and, therefore, required to report it, or if the prospect self-reports it, or if you can create an educated estimate based on the prospect's job title and location.

Another formula you could use is the following:

◆ Total real estate value +

◆ Total stock value +

◆ Other visible assets value +

◆ Salary

◆ = Total assets

> This is a fantastic book that you should have in your library! A companion, *Millionaire Women Next Door*, also provides great commentary about these individuals.
>
> practical tip

If the prospect is under 65, then the capacity is approximately ten to fifteen percent of the total amount. If the prospect is over 65, then the capacity might be closer to thirty to thirty-five percent of the total amount.

> Remember that capacity is not the same as affinity. Just because a prospect CAN give you forty percent of net worth doesn't mean the prospect will be inclined to do so. For a discussion of affinity, refer back to the chapter "Basic Connection(s) to Your Organization."
>
> **watch out!**

According to IRS statistics, real estate holdings generally represent twenty percent of a prospect's total wealth portfolio. This rule applies *only* to people in higher income brackets, or "the wealthy." How you define *wealthy* depends heavily on the area you live in (e.g., big city vs. farm country).

Another general formula based on real estate is that a prospect whose home is worth $500,000 can give in the $50,000 gift range. And with a $1 million home value, a prospect can likely give in the $100,000 gift range. This formula varies greatly in cities and areas with higher-than-average home values and does not apply in the same ratio anywhere the home value is below $500,000. And it is often possible that prospects with home values above $1 million have enough other assets that giving capacity grows exponentially and is no longer tied to home value.

Another common approach is to ask for a gift of one to two percent of a prospect's total net worth. Or sometimes one to two percent of a prospect's annual income. This is a very general formula though and, again, we highly recommend tailoring your ask to the specific details you have on and about the prospect.

Net Worth Cautionary Tale

You may have seen the following email on the PRSPCT-L listserve in early 2012, yet we contacted Valerie to get her permission to include it here as well. Sometimes you need to step out of the "prospect research" box and step into the box of "reality" when you're talking about net worth.

> Remember that when we're talking about net worth, we are *always* talking about a range. There is no way we can know everything about anyone's financial situation, but we can use the information we have to make educated assumptions about the range of wealth a prospect likely has.
>
>
> **! important**

What's interesting about the CNN [net worth] calculator is that it provides you with comparative data based on your age and income, rather than the Stanley/Danko model (above), which provides no context (although we would assume that it is based on certain assumptions about the cumulative effect of assets and income). CNN's data comes from Nielson/Claritas (noted on the site), which is an industry aggregator, and my understanding (which may be outdated) is that most of that comes from consumer marketing survey data and pooled industry feeds (I also have seen it work pretty handily in some nondevelopment situations).

Examples, though, are always handy (numbers changed to protect the innocent):

Let's say that you're a 47-year-old suburban mom fighting midriff bulge (like me) making $80,000 a year.

Stanley/Danko tells you that my "net worth" is $376,000.

CNN says that for my income bracket, the "median" net worth is $301,475, which means that according to Stanley/Danko, I'm 24.7 percent above the median! Wow!

Now let's think about a college classmate of mine, also 47, but probably fighting midriff with a trainer, whose annual income is easily $580,000.

Stanley/Danko would say that my classmate's "net worth" is $2,726,000.

CNN says that that income bracket's "median" is $1,122,900, making my classmate 142.7 percent above the median.

Interestingly, though, if my classmate's income was twice as much, more like $1,080,000, CNN's "median" would still be $1,122,900, but Stanley/Danko's formula would reflect that increase by estimating his "net worth" at $5,076,000.

Ah! See that?

In my experience, the best "net worth" rating is like trying on pants. They all look good on the rack. But you have to read the label to see what they're made of, then pull them on and walk around in them a bit, and take in the rest of the picture, until you can determine what is a fair estimate for the prospect in question. You also might need to tinker, and your eye gets better the more you do this sort of thing. [emphasis ours]

The lesson, though, is knowing as much as you can about the prospect before attempting a wealth rating. I know everything about my financial situation (home equity, savings, etc.) so the range provided by CNN and Stanley/Danko seems like a pretty reasonable estimate. I also understand a bit more about my classmate than what the calculators see, and I feel pretty confident that all estimates are ridiculously low.

Man, the stuff I wish I knew in college . . .

Best regards,

Valerie Anastasio

Broad Institute

To Recap

◆ Gift capacity helps determine appropriate asks.

◆ Gift capacity calculations are always estimates.

Chapter Twenty-Two

Profiling Middle of the Road Prospects

IN THIS CHAPTER

···→ Components of a profile for Middle of the Road Prospects

···→ Suggested layout for expanded profile

W e're halfway through our giving pyramid now and have learned about many of the components of a successful research profile. In the first part of this manual, we learned about foundational prospects and how to identify connections to the organization, contact information, and different forms of giving to get an initial picture of the prospects. In this part, we learned some more detailed information about how to delve deeper into major gift territory.

The preceding five chapters taught us how to expand our information and look more in depth at more affluent prospects. In the template in this chapter, we give you headings for the next five sections of the profile. In addition to what you learned in the first part of the book, we now have sections to denote real estate holdings, affiliations with various boards, and committees that will help you network between prospects, relationships with family and other colleagues, personal and shared interests, and capacity range estimates.

When you're looking at a middle of the road prospect, you can start to expand on the idea of capacity range for major gifts, but it's important to remember that the relationship comes first, which is why this section is last.

Sample Template for Middle of the Road Prospect

Section 1: Connections to Our University

- ❑ Alumnus (When was graduation? More than one degree? What field?)
- ❑ Parent (To whom?)
- ❑ Board member
- ❑ Student
- ❑ Volunteer (With what programs?)
- ❑ Employee (In what department/s?)
- ❑ Former employee (When was retirement or resignation?)
- ❑ Specific names of individual connections within our institution
- ❑ Other connections

Section 2: Contact Information

- ❑ Street address, city, and state of primary home address
- ❑ Street address, city, and state of any additional residences (If these are seasonal, do you have dates when the individual tends to be at these addresses?)
- ❑ Street address, city, and state of primary business address
- ❑ Street address, city, and state of any additional business addresses (Owner of multiple businesses? Offices in more than one location?)
- ❑ Primary home phone number
- ❑ Primary personal cell phone number
- ❑ Primary business phone number
- ❑ Primary business cell number
- ❑ Primary personal email address
- ❑ Primary business address
- ❑ Notation about which contact preferred

Section 3: General Philanthropy

- ❑ Gifts above $5,000: Organization (Location), Year
- ❑ Gifts between $1,000 and $4,999: Organization (Location), Year
- ❑ Gifts between $500 and $999: Organization (Location), Year
- ❑ Gifts between $100 and $499: Organization (Location), Year
- ❑ Gifts up to $99: Organization (Location), Year
- ❑ Unspecified Amount Gifts: Organization (Location), Year

Section 4: Political Giving

- ❑ Candidate, Year, Amount, Type
- ❑ Party Registration

Section 5: Real Estate

- ❑ Primary home address: date purchased, market value, APN, notes
- ❑ Additional property address(es): date purchased, market value, APN, notes
- ❑ Total number of properties owned
- ❑ Market value range of all properties

Section 6: Affiliations, Boards, and Committees

- ❑ Nonprofit name (years of participation), affiliation
- ❑ Committee type, nonprofit name, (year of participation)

Section 7: Family and Significant Relationships/Legacy Families

- ❑ Family member name, relationship, birth date, deceased date, address
- ❑ Relationships to others in our database: name, ID number, relationship

Section 8: Personal and Shared Interests

- ❑ Hobbies noted
- ❑ Interests identified

Section 9: Capacity Range

- ❑ General capacity range for a stretch gift over five years to top charity or group of charities: (amount, source)
- ❑ Additional capacity range estimates or rationale: (amount, source, notes)

Hopefully you are now starting to see the prospect profile take shape! You can really get a great picture of who the prospect is and provide some good details to frontline fundraisers to build relationships with the prospects by filling in as many of these sections as possible.

To Recap

- ◆ Middle of the road (major gifts) prospects get detailed profiles to inform relationships.

- ◆ Provide capacity estimates only after providing affiliations, relationships, and general information.

- ◆ Make sure your template builds on what you completed previously.

Part Four

The Big Leagues

The Big Leagues are a fun place to hang out! These are the people who can afford the things most of us only dream about. This means, of course, that you might be able to learn a whole lot of information, or you might not be able to find much at all, because these are typically very savvy investors who know what needs to be public information and what can remain private information.

I like to watch television shows such as "Selling New York" and "Selling L.A." to see how these folks live, because it is so different from my life (and probably yours too if you are researching them for your nonprofit organization). These people buy and sell real estate as an investment, not just for a place to live.

In chapter 23 through chapter 27, we look at how prospect researchers learn about their donors at this level and provide tips about where to find information on public stock holdings, assets, luxury items, salaries, and professional data.

4 The Big Leagues
- Stocks
- Salary • Company
- Franchises
- Charitable Foundation
- Luxury Items

3 - Middle of the Road
- Real Estate • Affiliations
- Family • Interests • Capacity

2 - Foundational Prospects
- Connections • Contacts
- Demographics & Public Records
- General Philanthropy & Political Giving

1 - Foundations
- Database • Templates • Glossary • Resources
- Data Mining & Predictive Modeling • Ethics and Laws
- Pyramids & Ranking • Bonus Features

Chapter Twenty-Three

Stocks

IN THIS CHAPTER

···➔ Who owns stock

···➔ How to find and value stock

By the time you get to your Big Leagues prospects, the likelihood that they hold a stock portfolio is pretty high. They are very often at the executive level of the company, or they might even run or own it. Or, like most people with any kind of wealth, they have made investments in the stock market. So researching and finding this data will be very helpful in determining giving capacity.

Company Insiders

If your prospect is an *insider* in a publicly traded company, you will be able to find out how much stock your prospect owns by using various sources on the web.

An *insider* is always one of the following:

◆ One of the top decision-making executives in a public company

◆ A beneficial owner, which means they own more than five percent of the total stock available for a public company

---

Use the stock research service you like. There are many available, and they all have benefits. The important thing, though, is to *be consistent* about which source you choose, since there can be slight degrees of variability from one source to the next.

practical tip

If someone is an insider in any particular company, looking at the insider roster in many cases also allows you to see a prospect's stock holdings in many public companies, in addition to the one you know about. This can be a very good way to estimate a person's total wealth holdings.

The services below use the insider roster of individuals who own significant shares of stock in the company.

- ◆ Yahoo Finance (finance.yahoo.com)

- ◆ Wall Street Journal Marketwatch (marketwatch.com)

- ◆ Google Finance (google.com/finance)

- ◆ Nasdaq (nasdaq.com)

- ◆ Reuters (reuters.com)

- ◆ marketbrief.com

- ◆ investing.msn.money.com

- ◆ money.cnn.com

- ◆ sec.gov/edgar/searchedgar/ companysearch.html (Forms def-14a will show executive compensation tables.)

You never know when a prospect might mention how a stock portfolio is doing. This is a great item to remind your gift officers to pass along to you if they hear it in passing. If the conversation frequently switches to topics of declining or rising stock prices, see whether they mention any specific stocks they own—or have owned for a long time. These kinds of mentions can provide you with a great deal of information to use when assessing the range of a prospect's net worth.

You *cannot* find stock information for anyone and everyone who owns stock by using the public information sources on the Internet. They must be insiders in a public company—this requires them to report stock information in that company to the Securities and Exchange Commission (SEC) for regulatory purposes. Even for people who are insiders, you cannot find everything they own, only the stocks held in public companies in which they are insiders.

important

John Jones is an executive with a start-up company called ABC Company. He also owns stock in two other companies. His stock portfolio in public companies looks like this:

ABC Company:

6,276 directly held shares x $33.98 (price as of 01/01/2012 4:45 p.m. EST) = $213,259

XYZ Company:

5,400 directly held shares x $98.40 (price as of 01/01/2012 5:30 p.m. EST) = $531,360

HLT Company

250,000 directly held shares x $104.80 (price as of 01/01/2012 3:45 p.m. EST) = $26,200,000

Mr. Jones' total stock holdings are valued at $26,944,619.

Example

Calculating Value of Stock Holdings

So, once you know a prospect's total holdings in any given company, find out the current price of the stock and multiply the total number of *directly held shares* by the current price.

For example:

6,276 directly held shares x $33.98 (price as of 01/01/2012 4:45 p.m. EST) = $213,259

As you can see, company insider rosters can provide researchers with a lot of important wealth information about our Big Leagues prospects.

Some subscription services (iWave PRO is one) can also deliver email alerts, daily or weekly, to your inbox with a list of new insider trades by executives that you designate. These alerts can tell you a lot about liquid wealth that your prospects own (when they sell off large amounts of stock, for example) in addition to wealth they have on paper within the stock market.

Directly held shares are stocks held in a prospect's name and are not restricted from sale. These shares can be sold for cash at any time or can be gifted to your organization.

VS.

Indirectly held shares have some kind of restriction on them—they are part of either a 401(k)/retirement plan or a trust or mutual fund, such that the prospect's name is not directly attached to it. Selling or gifting these shares is not possible, so we do not count them toward a prospect's capacity.

To Recap

◆ Insider stock information is a key wealth indicator.

◆ Set up alerts for prospect stock transactions.

Chapter Twenty-Four

Salary and Professional Information

IN THIS CHAPTER

> ---→ Finding salary and professional information

> ---→ Using salary information to determine capacity

So now let's turn our asset discussion to salary and professional information. While it's not always publicly available, there are a lot of ways you can determine a salary range for your Big League prospects. And it is yet another piece of data that you can use to estimate giving capacity.

Locating Salary Data

If your prospect is one of the top-five executives at a large public company, salary will be easy to find! They are required to file executive compensation data as part of annual tax statements. You will find this information in Form def-14a of the prospect's tax returns, which is available from the Securities and Exchange Commission (SEC). You can often also find this information in annual reports available on company websites.

The best place to find Form def-14a is to go straight to the source, the SEC's website, also known as EDGAR. We listed it above, but it's worthwhile enough to list again, here: sec.gov/edgar/searchedgar/companysearch.html.

If you are in Canada, there are similar sites called SEDI and SEDAR where you can search for this information.

I worked for Bradley University, which is located in Peoria, Illinois, the same city where Caterpillar's world headquarters is located (the heavy machinery company, in case you didn't know). Every year, the local newspaper published an article listing the top executives and their salary and stock information—shortly after Cat's annual report came out. It would break down the data into simple, easily accessible language. The news article made my job a lot easier. Most of my fundraising officers knew about it too, and they made sure to read it themselves.

So take a look around your town or region for similar articles—in newspapers, business journals, and such. If your city or area has a large segment of the population employed at this kind of public company, like they do in Peoria, it's very likely you'll find this for yourself.

Following are other helpful web sources for salary data:

◆ salary.com

◆ monster.com

◆ careerbuilder.com

◆ salarylist.com

Look for a press release about a new position in one of the top executive spots, and you are likely to find a significant amount of information about salary and bonus structure (and probably stock options too) and potentially other information as well.

A recent press release for a new CEO provided a list of starting salary, bonus structure for five years (and requirements to achieve them), stock options, stock vesting period, significant professional achievements and goals, and career history.

You can use the sites above to get an estimated salary range for your prospect's job title in a geographic area. You might want to check a few different sites and similar job titles and create an average salary range to get the most accurate estimate.

Using Salary to Calculate Net Worth

If you can find an exact salary, or make a pretty solid guess at what it is, you can use salary to determine an estimated gift level. The most common formula is to consider a gift level of one to two percent of annual salary. But, as we've said before, this is just a guess. We recommend considering all pieces of the prospect's wealth picture in putting together your gift puzzle.

It is important when using salary as part of the process of determining net worth, to consider *where* the prospect lives. The cost-of-living index can make a huge difference in the buying power of money.

ZipSkinny (zipskinny.com) is a useful resource for this data that will offer you a lot of other factors as well, including median income, education level, population statistics, and more. It will let you compare a specific zip code with up to twenty others, so you can gain a relative understanding of the neighborhood where your prospect lives.

To Recap

◆ Finding salary and professional information helps build a prospect's wealth profile.

◆ Use salary data to estimate gift capacity.

Chapter Twenty-Five

Prospect Company Information and Research

IN THIS CHAPTER

···→ Types of companies your prospects may own

···→ Where to find corporate and business assets

···→ Franchises

This chapter focuses on researching corporate or business information related to individual prospects. This provides a different perspective from researching the companies *as donors*. In this chapter, we will discuss what information about a prospect's company is useful and how it relates to ability to give to your organization.

Categories of Business Ownership/Leadership

Usually, the company and your prospect's place in it falls into one or more of the following categories, and each will mean a slightly different thing to your researching the person's wealth within that company.

◆ The company is very small, and just one person owns the business.

◆ The company is rather small, and the prospect is a partial owner (probably one-half, one-third, or potentially one-fourth, but not usually more than that).

◆ The prospect owns or is an executive at a large corporation.

◆ The prospect owns other companies or franchises.

Start-Ups

If your prospect is an entrepreneur who owns one or two small start-up companies, there is a good likelihood that most funds are tied up within the business(es). However, a franchise owner or owner of a large corporation has probably passed by the initial hurdles of business ownership and you can be more confident in the valuation of the company for these individuals.

Public Companies

Without a doubt, public companies are the easiest to research. The information is available to you, and you just need to make some sense of it. You will find information from the SEC, or the various finance pages listed in the chapter on stocks above, or on the website for the company itself.

Private Companies

Private companies are significantly more challenging. You will most likely learn only what they choose to tell you on the company's own website or in an annual report, or you may find nothing at all! A great place to start, though, is a business librarian at a facility near you. Or you could take a class in private company valuation through a college or university library school program (many offer these classes online as well) or check out some of the webinars archived on APRA's website (aprahome.org).

Locating Corporate Information

Useful asset information for companies:

- ◆ annual sales (try to acquire more than a few years of sales to see the direction of the trend-line)

- ◆ approximate size and number of employees and/or locations

- ◆ stock prices (again, look at the trend line to help with forecasting)

- ◆ shares outstanding

- ◆ profits

- ◆ margin on sales/profits

- ◆ board members (this circles back to the networks and contacts topics covered earlier—critical links in business—so it's good if we can understand them as well when interacting with individuals from these companies)

Find below some great websites for corporate research:

- ◆ marketresearch.com

- ◆ faqs.org

- ◆ bbb.org

- ◆ manta.com

- ◆ foundationsearch.com

- ◆ hoovers.com

If you don't quite understand how to read all of the corporate financial statements, find a copy of a finance or accounting textbook (probably from an introductory-level course) that explains terminology and process as well as the impact that various items have on the overall financial health of the company.

practical tip

You will often find your prospect listed on the Dun & Bradstreet business registrations, which might be your first indication that the prospect owns a company. A research profile from subscription sites like Wealth Engine or Target Analytics often provides you many of these listings for a name that matches your prospect, and you will need to determine which are truly correct.

Franchises

Commonly shared wisdom or insight about franchises, in regard to income and wealth, is that if a prospect owns one franchise, the prospect is probably working long hours, and most of the prospect's money and time is wrapped up in that one business. If a prospect owns two, things are a little easier. If they a prospect owns three or more—that's probably the prospect you want to look at!

Once a person has achieved ownership of, or invested in, three or more franchise locations, that individual is able to share resources among those businesses—employees, managers, supplies, etc., and is sitting at the top of that income and resource pile. That person is behind the scenes managing it all, without having to get into the kitchen when a cook or a cashier calls in sick or drive across the state to get more supplies if they suddenly run out.

Finding information online to confirm ownership of franchises can be tricky, but it's out there. You'll need to look through

If you don't find a company you're looking for in one of the search sources, don't totally give up on it. Look in some other sources, and you might find a different name and can then go back to the first source and try that. For example, I looked up company BEAN and did not find it in Wealth Engine. However, in Zoominfo, I found a blurb that said "BEAN, which used to be known as Brightstar External Analog Networks . . ." So I went back to Wealth Engine and was able to find a profile for the company under the name "Brightstar External Analog Networks."

practical tip

Every state is different, and corporate regulations might be under a different division. Or this information might not be available online at all. Once you do find the business information site for your state, or a state you look in frequently, bookmark it!

important

your local government business or corporate records. These records are usually compiled at the state level, so try to find your state's business and corporate regulatory division. For example, in Illinois, the Secretary of State handles this function, and you can search for businesses by name at the state website, ilsos. gov/corporatellc.

Very often, people who own a number of franchise businesses have incorporated all of them under some other name than the actual business. For example, your prospect might own six or seven McDonald's franchises. But the corporation under which the prospect has put them all, as one business unit, isn't called simply "McDonald's." That name is taken.

So what name is it under? Hopefully you already know that or your fundraising officer has given you that piece of information. Because the possibilities are endless. The prospect might use initials—for example, John Q. Doe runs his McDonald's under JQD Enterprises. Or it's named after the kids. Or the dog. Or just about anything you can think of!

If you are lucky, you can search your prospect's state corporation database by owner or officer name. Or maybe by the address of one location that you know your prospect owns. Try to find the one thing you can search by to confirm the name of the company, and go from there.

This information is also available in the corporate search section if you subscribe to LexisNexis for Development Professional, Wealth Engine, or the like.

To Recap

◆ The type of business a prospect owns or runs can help inform the prospect's wealth profile.

◆ Pick your favorite sites to find business or corporate data.

◆ It is key to know how many franchise operations a prospect owns or runs.

Chapter Twenty-Six

Family Foundations and Private Foundations

IN THIS CHAPTER

···→ The importance of foundation information

···→ Where to find foundation records

Family and private foundations are vehicles donors use to distribute their wealth to organizations that are important to them or are doing things that align with the prospect's own values. This chapter examines how these foundations fit in with our work as researchers for nonprofits.

Benefits of Foundation Data

If you are researching a family foundation, you might be able to find out how your prospect or prospect's family members contribute, and at what level, to the total assets of the foundation. This is another way to determine the assets of your prospect or family members.

It is also possible that your fundraisers can approach the family foundation for a gift to your organization. You will want to read through the foundation's IRS Form 990 to see how and to what organizations they make donations.

If the prospect has a family foundation, that is a good indication that the prospect has quite a few assets. Even if you don't know how much, it's a good thing to know that a private foundation exists.

Locating Foundation Information

Family foundations and other private foundations may be difficult to locate, but there are several sources at our disposal.

Sources for foundation information:

- ◆ Guidestar.com

- ◆ FoundationCenter.org (Foundation Directory Online)

- ◆ FoundationSearch.com (subscription)

- ◆ iWave PRO (subscription, contains Guidestar 990s)

- ◆ IRS (irs.gov/charities/article/0,,id=249767,00.html)

With these sources, you can often enter the prospect's name or partial name to locate whether a family foundation exists. Once you locate the foundation, you can search for its 990 forms to determine total assets held by the foundation. The document will perhaps give you the major contributions received by the foundation, including which family members contributed within the year.

Foundations are often required to file IRS 990-PF forms that list their holdings in other companies, giving you some indication of the assets under their management, even if it's not listed in the "stocks" section or insider trading. They will be required to list the earnings on their assets and investments as income on balance sheets.

A 990 will often also list the size of grants awarded and to whom they were given, providing you another way to determine whether your organization lines up with your prospect's philanthropic interests.

To Recap

- ◆ Charitable foundations are a solid indicator of wealth and philanthropic interest.

- ◆ Find out everything you can about a prospect's foundations.

Chapter Twenty-Seven

Luxury Items

IN THIS CHAPTER

···→ Luxury items to watch out for

···→ Some resources for finding luxury item values

Luxury items might be one of the first factors people think of when they consider someone in the Big Leagues. For many of these individuals, wealth is not a commodity, but rather a lifestyle. And the items you own convey how luxurious that lifestyle is.

Identifying Luxury

You may or may not be able to determine the actual value of luxury items owned by your prospect. However, knowing which luxury items your prospect owns can be very helpful when attempting to gauge net worth and potential available assets.

I have been told by many a boat owner that "a boat is just a hole in the water that you pour your money into," with the implication that it gives you zero return on investment. The same thinking applies to horses. Even if your prospect races and/or breeds them, unless that horse is at the top of the ranks, it will return only enough money to break even on costs and care, if you are lucky.

What I'm saying here is that boats and horses represent significant investments with little to no ROI, and it means that your prospect has *significant* disposable income to spend on such nonessential items. And, therefore, probably enough money to also give your organization a nice major gift.

Example

Items you might want to look for:

- private airplanes

- boats

- very high-end cars or multiple high-end cars

- horses (if you find this, make sure to make a note of it!)

- artwork and collections

When using luxury items to estimate net worth of a prospect, make a list of what the prospect owns and the quantity. If you come across the value of any of these items, note them as well.

Valuing Luxury

Following are a few great sites for finding estimated values of luxury items:

Art

- artnet.com may be good option for recent auction pricing.

- artfact.com may be good option for recent auction pricing.

Q: Hey, what do you do about someone who doesn't appear to have a whole lot of visible money (capacity may be five figures) but legend has it they have a multimillion-dollar art collection? People have seen said artwork, but none have written what's included.

A: We have both had this happen a few times. And both of us had to look pretty darn hard for some kind of information about the artwork/collection.

It's best to start by searching the Internet for instances where they have loaned it to a museum or organization. You can do this by Googling the name like you would look for donations: "Mr. and Mrs. Joseph M. Smith." Maybe add the words "loaned," or "collection," or "gallery" to narrow your search.

Q: But I think that they just have it at home, though it is pretty extensive . . .

A: Then I'd look for media or Internet articles, like mentions in *House Beautiful* or local area magazines that feature fancy homes. That's how I found this information for a prospect in Florida—from an otherwise obscure magazine article that mentioned his collection briefly in a larger profile of the prospect.

It is a great idea to encourage development officers to take note of such luxury items when they meet with prospects. If while visiting at a prospect's home, an officer notices original or reproduction Picasso or Monet paintings or notices that the prospect drives a Rolls Royce to the meeting—definitely encourage the officer to bring that information back to you. An officer will also notice if the prospect mentions luxury items that are owned.

practical tip

Fundraisers have come to me with information about some unusual collections—once about a collection of wooden model airplanes. Another time, rare books. Some items are nearly impossible for you to value, and so valuation is best left to an expert.

If your prospect (or the late prospect's family) wants to donate the collection to your organization or wants to sell the collection and donate the proceeds to you, it is common practice to hire an expert to value, and even sell, the collection for both parties. This can be paid for from the proceeds of the sale. If the collection is being donated, then it is in your best interest, and required for tax purposes, to get a formal valuation or appraisal of the collection.

stories from the real world

Airplanes

- ◆ landings.com

- ◆ registry.faa.gov/aircraftinquiry/state_inquiry.asp

Boats

- ◆ shiplink.info

- ◆ yachtsalvage.com

- ◆ yachtworld.com

Cars

- ◆ kbb.com

To Recap

- ◆ Owning luxury items indicates wealth.

- ◆ Stay on the lookout for ever-evolving resources for luxury item values.

Chapter Twenty-Eight

Profiling Prospects in the Big Leagues

IN THIS CHAPTER

⋯➤ Components of the full profile for Big League Prospects

⋯➤ Suggested layout for full profile

We've reached the end of our prospect research journey now, and it seems fitting to explore the components of the full profile template now. It's helpful to remember that in bygone days, the full prospect profile could be ten to twenty pages (or more!) in length and really told a story about the donor in a narrative fashion. Now, most often we don't need to provide a lot of narration with our information, but we still need to get the story across. The template included here shows you all fourteen of the sections we advocate in this manual, along with some notes about the types of details to include in each section. Of course you will want to tailor this presentation to the needs of your organization and the people for whom you are providing the profiles.

In the last five chapters, we spent some time discussing the types of financial information that pretty much only apply to prospects in really high giving capacity groups. The first section added to our profile here is about stocks and other financial assets. Second, you will see in section 11 that we now encounter prospects for whom we can find salary and income information. It is likely that big leagues prospects are top executives in companies, and their information is, therefore, public. Following that, information about their business or company ownership will apply when you're researching prospects in this segment, and they are the most likely to have a private or family foundation. Finally, the last section in our full profile template offers you a place to make notes about any luxury items you discover. While some luxury items are a drain on finances, it's also true that simply owning many expensive items can denote some level of discretionary wealth and therefore it should be included here.

Sample Template for Big League Prospect

Section 1: Connections to Our University

- ❑ Alumnus (When was graduation? More than one degree? What field?)
- ❑ Parent (To whom?)
- ❑ Board member
- ❑ Student
- ❑ Volunteer (With what programs?)
- ❑ Employee (In what department/s?)
- ❑ Former employee (When was retirement or resignation?)
- ❑ Specific names of individual connections within our institution
- ❑ Other connections

Section 2: Contact Information

- ❑ Street address, city, and state of primary home address
- ❑ Street address, city, and state of any additional residences (If these are seasonal, do you have dates when the individual tends to be at these addresses?)
- ❑ Street address, city, and state of primary business address
- ❑ Street address, city, and state of any additional business addresses (Owner of multiple businesses? Offices in more than one location?)
- ❑ Primary home phone number
- ❑ Primary personal cell phone number
- ❑ Primary business phone number
- ❑ Primary business cell number
- ❑ Primary personal email address
- ❑ Primary business address
- ❑ Notation about which contact preferred

Section 3: General Philanthropy

- ❑ Gifts above $5,000: Organization (Location), Year
- ❑ Gifts between $1,000 and $4,999: Organization (Location), Year
- ❑ Gifts between $500 and $999: Organization (Location), Year

❏ Gifts between $100 and $499: Organization (Location), Year

❏ Gifts up to $99: Organization (Location), Year

❏ Unspecified Amount Gifts: Organization (Location), Year

Section 4: Political Giving

❏ Candidate, Year, Amount, Type

❏ Party Registration

Section 5: Real Estate

❏ Primary home address: date purchased, market value, APN, notes

❏ Additional property address(es): date purchased, market value, APN, notes

❏ Total number of properties owned

❏ Market value range of all properties

Section 6: Affiliations, Boards, and Committees

❏ Nonprofit name (years of participation), affiliation

❏ Committee type, nonprofit name, (year of participation)

Section 7: Family and Significant Relationships/Legacy Families

❏ Family member name, relationship, birth date, deceased date, address

❏ Relationships to others in our database: name, ID number, relationship

Section 8: Personal and Shared Interests

❏ Hobbies noted

❏ Interests identified

Section 9: Capacity Range

❏ General capacity range for a stretch gift over five years to top charity or group of charities: (amount, source)

❏ Additional capacity range estimates or rationale: (amount, source, notes)

Section 10: Stocks and Other Financial Assets

❏ Total holdings

❏ Ticker symbol, number direct shares, dollar value of shares at date/time

Section 11: Salary and Income Information

❏ Estimated salary range

❏ Bonus structure

❏ Additional compensation notes

Section 12: Company/Business Information

- ❑ Category of ownership/leadership
- ❑ Annual sales
- ❑ Approximate size and number of employees
- ❑ Stock prices
- ❑ Board members
- ❑ Subsidiaries and/or parent companies

Section 13: Family and Private Foundations

- ❑ Total assets
- ❑ Board members
- ❑ Grant application guidelines
- ❑ Grants awarded: amount, beneficiary, year
- ❑ Other important information

Section 14: Luxury Items

- ❑ Item, value, notes
- ❑ Size of collection(s)
- ❑ Note of ownership of more than one luxury item
- ❑ Notes from contact reports about potential ownership

Well, there you have it: the full profile template! It's the essence of all the information you've learned throughout this manual, put into bullet-point form for quick consumption and implementation in your organization. Though you are free to move sections around to suit your needs, we suggest them in the order given because of how each section builds upon the ones before it and helps complete the full picture of the prospect.

To Recap

- ◆ Always take time for a full profile for Big League prospects.

- ◆ Remember foundational information is still necessary for full profiles.

- ◆ Full profiles are data rich but provided in nugget form.

Epilogue

Well, hopefully you have enjoyed the journey you've just taken with us through the prospect research campaign pyramid. We spent a lot of time attending to the details of foundations and resources, because they are SO fundamental to success in this field. By laying the information out in the way we did, hopefully you are able to follow how each of the pieces is built upon, but independent of, the pieces that came before it. You won't likely need the "Big Leagues" data for an annual fund ask, but you will need the foundational data at some point as you're building a relationship toward a Big League ask.

In the appendices that follow, we give you several additional resources, including a resource list with books, reports, professional associations, subscription services, screening services, blogs, Internet sources for specific types of data, Codes of Ethics from AFP, APRA, and AASP, as well as the Donor Bill of Rights. We wish you good luck and happy searching. And we hope to meet you at a conference one day.

Appendix A

Resources

Further Reading

These are texts you should definitely check out if you're working in prospect research:

◆ Birkolz, Joshua. *Fundraising Analytics: Using Data to Guide Strategy*. Wylie, 2008.

◆ Hogan, Cecelia. *Prospect Research, a Primer for Growing Nonprofits, 2nd edition*. Boston: Jones & Bartlett Publishers, 2008.

◆ Wylie, Peter. *Data Mining for Fundraisers*. Washington, DC: CASE, 2004.

Reports

These reports offer insightful information about trends in various aspects of philanthropy on a national and global scale:

◆ Giving USA—this is a wealth of information on philanthropy in the United States put out annually by the Giving USA Foundation and the Center on Philanthropy at Indiana University. Go to givingusareports.org to check it out and download or order copies.

◆ Bank of America High Net Worth Philanthropy studies (October 2006, 2010)— These are a result of a collaboration between Bank of America and the Center on Philanthropy at Indiana University. Go to mediaroom.bankofamerica.com/phoenix. zhtml?c=234503&p=mediaMention&id=394026 to learn more about these foundation studies of high net worth individuals in the United States.

◆ World Wealth Report—This study is annually compiled by Capgemini and Merrill Lynch Global Wealth Management and seeks to identify characteristics of high-net-worth individuals. Go to us.capgemini.com/worldwealthreport to learn more or download various reports.

◆ Geography and Giving Study: The Boston Foundation, June 2007—A report of philanthropy in New England put out by the Center on Philanthropy at Boston College. Go to bc.edu/research/cwp/features/geographyandgiving.html to download the report.

◆ VSE—Voluntary Support of Education, for educational institutions. This annual survey is completed by institutions nationwide, and results are compiled for comparison. You must be a participating member to log in to the website at vse.cae.org. Institutions that participate in the survey can access the summary results as well.

Associations

There are many great professional associations out there relevant to prospect research. Some you should be sure to consider:

◆ AASP—Association of Advancement Services Professionals (advserv.org)

◆ AFP—Association of Fundraising Professionals (afpnet.org)

◆ AHP—Association for Healthcare Philanthropy (ahp.org)

◆ APRA—Association of Professional Researchers for Advancement (aprahome.org)

◆ CASE—Council for Advancement and Support of Education (case.org)

◆ GPA—Grant Professionals Association, formerly American Association of Grant Professionals (AAGP) (grantprofessionals.org)

◆ RIF—Institute of Fundraising, Researchers in Fundraising (institute-of-fundraising.org.uk/groupsandnetworking/institutegroups/specialinterestgroups/researchersinfundraising)

Subscription Services

Some of the bigger names in prospect research services:

◆ Accurint (also known as AlumniFinder)—This company is owned by LexisNexis but also can be purchased separately with slightly different functionality (accurint.com).

◆ Foundation Center—For researching foundations and grants (foundationcenter.org).

◆ Foundation Search and Big Online—For researching foundations, grants, and philanthropy of really large national companies (foundationsearch.com).

◆ Investor Word of the Day/Week—I subscribe to this service, which gives me a stock market or accounting term, its definition, and other information about how the stock market is doing. It's helpful for background information about the economy and helpful to know what these words mean, because our big donors certainly do (investorwords.com).

◆ iWave Prospect Research Online (PRO)—For researching individuals, foundations, and companies. This service contains subscriptions to Zoominfo, Ctelligence (for donations), Guidestar, High Net Worth alert, HEP Giftsplusonline, a 990 search, and Pro Data (iWave.com).

◆ GuideStar—For Foundation 990s and other nonprofit information (guidestar.org).

◆ LexisNexis for Development Professionals—For researching individuals and corporations. You can find demographics, wealth, news, philanthropy, connections, and other public documents (academic.lexisnexis.com/development-professionals/lexisnexis-for-development-professionals/lndp-overview.aspx)

◆ Research Point (Target Analytics from Blackbaud)—For researching individuals. You can find wealth information, modeling, Noza donations, demographics, and more (blackbaud.com/targetanalytics/prospectresearch/researchmgmt/researchmgmt_ov.aspx).

Screening Services

Some of the bigger names in wealth screening services are found using these services:

◆ Blackbaud/Target Analytics (blackbaud.com)

◆ DonorSearch (donorsearch.net)

◆ DonorScape by Grenzebach Glier and Associates (grenzebachglier.com)

◆ DonorTrends, Inc. (donortrends.com)

◆ HEP Matching Gifts (hepdevelopment.com)

◆ MaGIC (majorgifts.net)

◆ Noza (nozasearch.com)

◆ Target America (tgtam.com)

◆ WealthEngine (wealthengine.com)

Books

These are some books that I have read and that have been recommended by other Researchers through the listserves :

◆ Ciconte, Barbara L. and Jeanne Jacob. *Fundraising Basics: A Complete Guide 3rd ed.* Boston: Jones & Bartlett Publishers, 2009.

◆ See Chapter Eight (p.137–145) on Prospect Research for understanding how research fits within the larger context of the development office.

◆ Frank, Robert. *Richistan.* New York: Crown Publishers, 2007.

◆ Hogan, Cecilia. *Prospect Research: A Primer for Growing Nonprofits 2nd ed.* Boston: Jones & Bartlett Publishers, 2008.

◆ Jordan, Ron and Katelyn L. Quynn. *Invest in Charity: A Donor's Guide to Charitable Giving.* New York: Wylie, 2001.

◆ Kaufman, Michael. *Soros: The Life and Times of a Messianic Billionaire.* New York: Knopf, 2002.

◆ Passell, Peter *How to Read the Financial Pages.* New York: Warner Books, 1998.

◆ Prince, Russ Alan and Karen Maru File. *The 7 Faces of Philanthropy.* San Francisco: Jossey-Bass, 1994.

◆ Reed II, A., K. Aquino, and E. Levy. "Moral Identity and Judgments of Charitable Behaviors." *Journal of Marketing* 71, no. 1, (2007): 178.

◆ Shang, J., A. Reed II, and R. Croson. "Identity Congruency Effects on Donations." *Journal of Marketing Research* 45, no. 3 (2008): 351–361.

◆ Solla, Laura A. *The Guide to Analyzing Wealth and Assets.* Freeport, PA: L.A. Solla, 2001.

◆ Solla, Laura. *The Guide to Prospect Research & Prospect Management* Freeport, PA: L.A. Solla, 2002 (available at researchprospects.com/Publications.html).

◆ Stanley, Thomas J. and William D. Danko. *The Millionaire Next Door: The Surprising Secrets of America's Wealthy.* Atlanta, GA: Longstreet Press, 1996.

◆ Stanley, Thomas J. *Millionaire Women Next Door.* Kansas City, MO: Andrews McMeel Publishing, 2004.

◆ Strand, Bobbie J. *A Kaleidoscope of Prospect Development: The Shapes and Shades of Major Donor Prospecting.* Washington, D.C.: CASE, 2008.

◆ Wylie, Peter B. *Data Mining for Fundraisers.* Washington, D.C.: CASE, 2004.

Philanthropy Blogs

No doubt there are countless great blogs out there, but these are two that I subscribe to:

◆ cooldata.wordpress.com

◆ prospectresearch.com

Web Resources for General Philanthropy

◆ alumnifinder.com (see information above about Accurint)

◆ multistatefiling.org for information on charity state registration requirements.

◆ LinkedIn—People's profiles often show up on a Google search, and you can find current and historical employer information here (use the public side only, do not sign into your own LinkedIn account to access additional information, as that could easily be a broach of privacy and ethics boundaries).

◆ Facebook—People's profiles often show up in a Google search, providing you clues to whether other sources you are looking at are for the correct person. A photo, for example, can be really helpful in some cases if you are trying to match a prospect to other profiles you find (use the public side only, do not sign into your own Facebook account to access additional information, unless your organization has a page and people can become fans—thus deliberately giving you access to information).

Physical Property Valuation

These resources are suggested by many researchers on the listserves as good places to begin to look when you're trying to estimate the value of physical property.

Art

◆ artnet.com may be good option for recent auction pricing

◆ artfact.com may be good option for recent auction pricing

◆ askart.com/AskART/index.aspx

Airplanes

◆ landings.com

◆ registry.faa.gov/aircraftinquiry/state_inquiry.asp

Boats

◆ abl-boats.com/index.pl

◆ boatsafe.com/nauticalknowhow/hin.html

◆ shiplink.info

◆ yachtsalvage.com

◆ yachtworld.com

Cars

◆ kbb.com

Political Contributions

◆ opensecrets.org/home/index.php Open Secrets

◆ Newsmeat.com records go back to the early 1980s (possibly earlier) and in many instances picks up federal, state, and local contributions

◆ moneyline.cq.com/pml/home.do

Real Estate

◆ realestate.yahoo.com/re/homevalues

◆ realtor.com

◆ luxuryrealestate.com

◆ residentialproperties.com

◆ zillow.com

◆ dataquick.com

◆ netronline.com

◆ pulawski.net, determining estimated market value of real estate from assessed value; includes links to property records from most states

◆ forbes.com/home/lists/2006/04/17/06zip_most-expensive-zip-codes_land.html Forbes most expensive zip codes

◆ money.cnn.com/pf/features/lists/million_zips/index.html CNN/Money Million Dollar zip codes

◆ money.cnn.com/pf/features/lists/high_income_zips/CNN/Money, six-figure zip codes

◆ images.businessweek.com/ss/07/04/0402_luxreapp/index_01.htm, Business Week richest zip codes

◆ bwnt.businessweek.com/interactive_reports/luxury_housing_special_report/index. asp, Business Week Luxury Housing Special Report

◆ realestate.msn.com

Salary Calculators

◆ salary.com

◆ salaryexpert.com

◆ careerjournal.com

◆ jobsmart.org/tools/salary/salarycalculator

◆ hoovers.com

◆ lexinexis.com

◆ bizstats.com for company valuation and compensation info

Business/Corporate Information

◆ corporateinformation.com

◆ motleyfool.com

◆ cbsmarketwatch.com

◆ manta.com, business background information

◆ theyrule.net, corporate board connections

◆ newsmeat.com NewsMeat, quick way to track down and find basic occupation information(job title and workplace) of major gift level donors who also make political contributions

◆ bvmarketdata.com, business valuation

◆ dnb.com/us/, Dun & Bradstreet

◆ factiva.com, DowJones information

◆ sec.gov/edgar/searchedgar/companysearch.html, SEC filings generally going back to 1994

◆ secinfo.com

◆ hoovers.com, Hoovers

◆ dnb.com/us, Dun & Bradstreet

◆ NNDB.com

◆ marketvisual.com

◆ forbes.com, Forbes

Relationship Mapping

◆ theyrule.net, corporate board connections for Board memberships for large companies in the United States

◆ muckety.com, Board memberships, though they have to be pretty high-level to show up here

◆ marketvisual.com, business relationship mapping

Birthdays

◆ birthdatabase.com/query.php

◆ stevemorse.org/birthday/birthday2.html

◆ anybirthday.com

Research Resource Lists

These sites compile and maintain resource lists for their Researchers. They can be terrific places to look when you're stumped about where to go.

◆ indorgs.virginia.edu/portico, wealth of information and research tools maintained by University of Virginia

◆ lambresearch.com,recommendations of research tools from David Lamb

◆ nudevelopment.com/research/bookmark.html, Northwestern University Prospect Research bookmarks

◆ AdvancementResearchToolkit.com/resources, Fitzgerald Information Services

Law Firms/Lawyers Information

◆ law.com, AM Law

◆ Martindale Hubbell directory, historical directory on law firm partners (access through LNDP)

◆ lawcrossing.com/lcjobresourcessalary.php, lawyer salaries by firm

International Research

There are countless sites on international research, and many of them change often. Be sure to check the listserves for information about specific countries you are researching. These are a few frequently suggested sources:

◆ gnosis.com.sg, International Screening: Gnosis, out of Singapore, specializing in this type of work for Asia

◆ sofii.org, knowledge sharing site out of the UK, called The Showcase of Fundraising Innovation and Inspiration (SOFII)

◆ mouseprice.com, Property records in the UK

◆ zoopla.co.uk, Property records in the UK

Stock Holdings

◆ In Canada, search for SEDI and SEDAR for stocks and filings

◆ In the United States, search for EDGAR and Yahoo Finance

◆ marketwatch.com/tools/quotes/insiders.asp, check on insider trading (click the NAME bullet)

◆ investopedia.com, background information that might be helpful to new researchers trying to make sense of SEC filings.

Ancestry Data

◆ rootsweb.com, social security death index

◆ legacy.com, free search for current obituaries; fee-based for past obituaries

◆ ancestry.com, information on families and histories

◆ bookoffamilytrees.com, updated monthly

◆ And never forget to check your local genealogy or history center, and/or the library. They usually have great resources and are more than happy to assist you.

Other Important Resources

◆ AFP Code of Ethics (reprinted below, or accessible at afpnet.org/Ethics)

◆ APRA Code of Ethics (reprinted below, or accessible at aprahome.org/ProfessionalStandards/StatementofEthics/tabid/74/Default.aspx)

◆ Donor Bill of Rights (reprinted below, or accessible at afpnet.org/Ethics)

◆ AASP Code of Ethics (reprinted below, or accessible at advserv.org/Default.aspx?pageId=90985)

◆ APRA Connections Magazine (available to APRA members)

◆ AASP Best Practices documents (available to APRA, AASP and ADRP members on the association websites)

◆ CASE Management and Reporting Standards (If you are an Education institution, these standards are vital for knowing what gifts to count and how to count them. If you're not an educational institution, it is still a very useful reference for campaign counting.)

◆ Listservs: Fundlist, Advance-L, Prospect-L, Prospect-DMM, Dataminers-L, Donor-Research-L, FundSVCS

◆ IRS Documents, primarily 526 and 1771, which are available at irs.gov

AFP Code of Ethics

AFP Code of Ethical Principles and Standards

ETHICAL PRINCIPALS (ADOPTED 1964; AMENDED SEPTEMBER 2007)

The Association of Fundraising Professionals (AFP) exists to foster the development and growth of fundraising professionals and the profession, to promote high ethical behavior in the fundraising profession and to preserve and enhance philanthropy and volunteerism. Members of AFP are motivated by an inner drive to improve the quality of life through the causes they serve. They serve the ideal of philanthropy, are committed to the preservation and enhancement of volunteerism, and hold stewardship of these concepts as the overriding direction of their professional lives. They recognize their responsibility to ensure that needed resources are vigorously and ethically sought and that the intent of the donor is honestly fulfilled. To these ends, AFP members, both individual and business, embrace certain values that they strive to uphold in performing their responsibilities for generating philanthropic support. AFP business members strive to promote and protect the work and mission of their client organizations.

AFP members both individual and business aspire to:

◆ Practice their profession with integrity, honesty, truthfulness, and adherence to the absolute obligation to safeguard the public trust.

◆ Act according to the highest goals and visions of their organizations, professions, clients, and consciences.

◆ Put philanthropic mission above personal gain.

◆ Inspire others through their own sense of dedication and high purpose.

◆ Improve their professional knowledge and skills so that their performance will better serve others.

◆ Demonstrate concern for the interests and well-being of individuals affected by their actions.

◆ Value the privacy, freedom of choice, and interests of all those affected by their actions.

◆ Foster cultural diversity and pluralistic values and treat all people with dignity and respect.

◆ Affirm, through personal giving, a commitment to philanthropy and its role in society.

◆ Adhere to the spirit as well as the letter of all applicable laws and regulations.

◆ Advocate within their organizations adherence to all applicable laws and regulations.

◆ Avoid even the appearance of any criminal offense or professional misconduct.

◆ Bring credit to the fundraising profession by their public demeanor.

◆ Encourage colleagues to embrace and practice these ethical principles and standards.

◆ Be aware of the codes of ethics promulgated by other professional organizations that serve philanthropy.

ETHICAL STANDARDS

Furthermore, while striving to act according to the above values, AFP members, both individual and business, agree to abide (and to ensure, to the best of their ability, that all members of their staff abide) by the AFP standards. Violation of the standards may subject the member to disciplinary sanctions, including expulsion, as provided in the AFP Ethics Enforcement Procedures.

MEMBER OBLIGATIONS

1. Members shall not engage in activities that harm the members' organizations, clients, or profession.

2. Members shall not engage in activities that conflict with their fiduciary, ethical, and legal obligations to their organizations, clients, or profession.

3. Members shall effectively disclose all potential and actual conflicts of interest; such disclosure does not preclude or imply ethical impropriety.

4. Members shall not exploit any relationship with a donor, prospect, volunteer, client, or employee for the benefit of the members or the members' organizations.

5. Members shall comply with all applicable local, state, provincial, and federal civil and criminal laws.

6. Members recognize their individual boundaries of competence and are forthcoming and truthful about their professional experience and qualifications and will represent their achievements accurately and without exaggeration.

7. Members shall present and supply products and/or services honestly and without misrepresentation and will clearly identify the details of those products, such as availability of the products and/or services and other factors that may affect the suitability of the products and/or services for donors, clients, or nonprofit organizations.

8. Members shall establish the nature and purpose of any contractual relationship at the outset and will be responsive and available to organizations and their employing organizations before, during, and after any sale of materials and/or services. Members will comply with all fair and reasonable obligations created by the contract.

9. Members shall refrain from knowingly infringing the intellectual property rights of other parties at all times. Members shall address and rectify any inadvertent infringement that may occur.

10. Members shall protect the confidentiality of all privileged information relating to the provider/client relationships.

11. Members shall refrain from any activity designed to disparage competitors untruthfully.

SOLICITATION AND USE OF PHILANTHROPIC FUNDS

12. Members shall take care to ensure that all solicitation and communication materials are accurate and correctly reflect their organizations' mission and use of solicited funds.

13. Members shall take care to ensure that donors receive informed, accurate and ethical advice about the value and tax implications of contributions.

14. Members shall take care to ensure that contributions are used in accordance with donors' intentions.

15. Members shall take care to ensure proper stewardship of all revenue sources, including timely reports on the use and management of such funds.

16. Members shall obtain explicit consent by donors before altering the conditions of financial transactions.

PRESENTATION OF INFORMATION

17. Members shall not disclose privileged or confidential information to unauthorized parties.

18. Members shall adhere to the principle that all donor and prospect information created by, or on behalf of, an organization or a client is the property of that organization or client and shall not be transferred or utilized except on behalf of that organization or client.

19. Members shall give donors and clients the opportunity to have their names removed from lists that are sold to, rented to, or exchanged with other organizations.

20. Members shall, when stating fundraising results, use accurate and consistent accounting methods that conform to the appropriate guidelines adopted by the American Institute of Certified Public Accountants (AICPA)* for the type of organization involved.

In countries outside of the United States, comparable authority should be utilized.

COMPENSATION AND CONTRACTS

21. Members shall not accept compensation or enter into a contract that is based on a percentage of contributions; nor shall members accept finder's fees or contingent fees. Business members must refrain from receiving compensation from third parties derived from products or services for a client without disclosing that third-party compensation to the client (for example, volume rebates from vendors to business members).

22. Members may accept performance-based compensation, such as bonuses, provided such bonuses are in accord with prevailing practices within the members' own organizations and are not based on a percentage of contributions.

23. Members shall neither offer nor accept payments or special considerations for the purpose of influencing the selection of products or services.

24. Members shall not pay finder's fees, commissions, or percentage compensation based on contributions, and shall take care to discourage their organizations from making such payments.

25. Any member receiving funds on behalf of a donor or client must meet the legal requirements for the disbursement of those funds. Any interest or income earned on the funds should be fully disclosed

APRA Code of Ethics

APRA Statement of Ethics (copyright © 2009 APRA revised December 2009)

PREAMBLE

Establishing and maintaining ethical and professional standards is a primary goal of the mission of the Association of Professional Researchers for Advancement (APRA). All APRA members shall support and further an individual's fundamental right to privacy and protect the confidential information of their institutions. All members agree to abide by this Statement of Ethics in the daily conduct of all professional activity encompassing the gathering, dissemination, and use of information for the purposes of fundraising or other institutional advancement activity.

Four fundamental principles provide the foundation for the ethical conduct of fundraising research, relationship management, and analytics: integrity, accountability, practice, and conflict of interest.

INTEGRITY

Members shall be truthful with respect to their identities and purpose and the identity of their institutions during the course of their work. They shall continually strive to increase the recognition and respect of the profession.

ACCOUNTABILITY

Members shall respect the privacy of donors and prospects and conduct their work with the highest level of discretion. They shall adhere to the spirit as well as the letter of all applicable laws and all policies of their organization. They shall conduct themselves in the utmost professional manner in accordance with the standards of their organization.

PRACTICE

Members shall take the necessary care to ensure that their work is as accurate as possible. They shall only record data that is appropriate to the fundraising process and protect the confidentiality of all personal information at all times.

CONFLICTS OF INTEREST

Members shall avoid competing professional or personal interests and shall disclose such interests to their institutions at the first instance. A conflict of interest can create an appearance of impropriety that can undermine confidence in the member, their organization, and the profession.

Donor Bill of Rights

The Donor Bill of Rights

Philanthropy is based on voluntary action for the common good. It is a tradition of giving and sharing that is primary to the quality of life. To ensure that philanthropy merits the respect and trust of the general public, and that donors and prospective donors can have full confidence in the nonprofit organizations and causes they are asked to support, we declare that all donors have these rights:

I. To be informed of the organization's mission, of the way the organization intends to use donated resources, and of its capacity to use donations effectively for their intended purposes.

II. To be informed of the identity of those serving on the organization's governing board, and to expect the board to exercise prudent judgment in its stewardship responsibilities.

III. To have access to the organization's most recent financial statements.

IV. To be assured their gifts will be used for the purposes for which they were given.

V. To receive appropriate acknowledgment and recognition.

VI. To be assured that information about their donation is handled with respect and with confidentiality to the extent provided by law.

VII. To expect that all relationships with individuals representing organizations of interest to the donor will be professional in nature.

VIII. To be informed whether those seeking donations are volunteers, employees of the organization or hired solicitors.

IX. To have the opportunity for their names to be deleted from mailing lists that an organization may intend to share.

X. To feel free to ask questions when making a donation and to receive prompt, truthful, and forthright answers.

AASP Code of Ethics (advserv.org/Default.aspx?pageId=90985)

Ethics Statement

Advancement Services Professionals, by virtue of their responsibilities within the advancement community, establish, affirm, and articulate the best standards of ethical practice, both as individuals and as members of professional staff at their respective nonprofit organizations. They have a special duty to exemplify the best qualities of their institutions and to observe the highest standards of personal and professional conduct. By example, Advancement Services professionals encourage their colleagues to embrace and practice these ethical principles and standards.

Confidentiality

They safeguard privacy rights and confidential information, balancing an individual's right to privacy with the needs of their institutions to collect, analyze, record, maintain, use, and disseminate information.

They follow the letter and spirit of laws and regulations safeguarding biographical and financial constituent data.

They observe these standards and others that apply to their profession and actively encourage colleagues to join them in supporting the highest standards of conduct regarding privacy rights and confidentiality.

Integrity

They are accountable to internal and external constituents, maintaining transparency and honesty.

They are responsible stewards of the resources (human, financial, capital, et al.) entrusted to their care.

They are committed to excellence and to maintaining the trust of their staff and constituency.

They respect the worth and dignity of individuals, recognizing their unique and valuable contributions at all levels within the Advancement organization, and demonstrate concern for the interests and well-being of individuals affected by their actions.

Service

They create positive interactions with internal and external constituents and offer the necessary tools and solutions to achieve the organization's fundraising goals and objectives. They continuously improve systems and procedures in their provision of professional services, resources, and solutions.

They partner with their peers to achieve the goals and objectives of the Advancement organization.

They maintain an ongoing commitment to quality, which is representative of the following attributes and traits: accountability, accuracy, attention to detail, creativity, confidentiality, conscientiousness, dedication, dependability, determination, efficiency, integrity, perseverance, respect, thoroughness, and timeliness.

They promote stewardship practices that are timely, personalized, sincere, creative, and flexible.

Practice

They establish metrics and monitor progress to ensure the accuracy and timeliness of all transactional data.

They abide by applicable government regulations and industry standards.

They maintain appropriate and consistent accounting, budgeting, and reporting methodologies.

They continuously pursue opportunities to enhance professional and personal skills, resulting in the highest levels of service to their donors and organizations; they seek out information and encourage their staff, at all levels, to pursue career development opportunities; and they share freely their knowledge and experience with others as appropriate.

They pursue progressive methods and modifications to improve conditions for, and benefits to, donors and their organization. They incorporate innovative management techniques leading to the highest level of efficiency in operations.

They maximize the utilization of technology in daily operations, particularly relative to information systems and data management.

They contribute to and employ best practices in all areas of Advancement Services.

This Statement of Ethics was compiled incorporating ideas and principles put forth in the following documents: CASE Statement of Ethics, Code of Ethical Principles and Standards—AFP, Statement of Ethics—APRA, AHP Statement of Professional Standards and Conduct, and the Independent Sector's Statement of Values and Code of Ethics for Nonprofit and Philanthropic organizations.

Index

If you enjoyed this book, you'll want to pick up the other books in the CharityChannel Press **In the Trenches™** series.

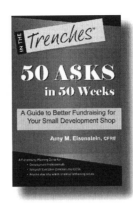

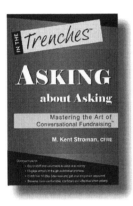

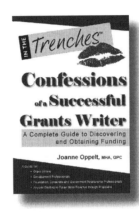

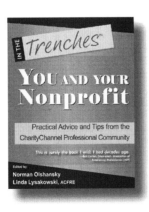

And dozens more coming soon!

www.CharityChannel.com

And now introducing **For the GENIUS® Press,** an imprint that produces books on just about any topic that people want to learn. You don't have to be a genius to read a **GENIUS** book, but you'll sure be smarter once you do!

Fundraising

for the GENIUS™

The only book you'll ever need to raise more money for your nonprofit organization.

FOR THE GENIUS IN ALL OF US™

Linda Lysakowski, ACFRE

www.ForTheGENIUS.com

PRESS

Made in the USA
San Bernardino, CA
24 November 2014